LO-FI MUSIC

Artistic Expression that Taps into Universal Human Experiences and Emotion

TERRY SMITH

Published by Otis Dynamic Enterprises

ISBN Paperback: 979-8-9915765-0-5
ISBN Ebook: 979-8-9915765-1-2

Printed in the United States of America

Also by Theresa Smith

Women In Football: Past Present and Future

CONTENTS

Introduction

Imagine a world where music isn't just heard but felt, where the familiar crackle of a vinyl record transports you to a place of serenity and nostalgia. This is the essence of lo-fi music—a genre that goes beyond mere sounds to evoke emotions and memories with its raw, unpolished charm. In our fast-paced, always-on lives, there's something profoundly soothing about music that embraces imperfection and simplicity, inviting us to slow down, breathe, and simply be.

Lo-fi music, short for "low fidelity," is all about celebrating those little imperfections that most other genres strive to erase. The gentle hiss of tape recordings, the subtle hum of background noise, and the cozy crackles are reminiscent of old records—these are not flaws but integral components of the lo-fi sound. They create an atmosphere that's both nostalgic and current, grounding listeners in a space where the past intertwines with the present.

This book explores the enigmatic origins of lo-fi music, tracing it back to its roots and following its evolution through the years. From its humble beginnings as a niche style embraced by underground artists, Lo-fi has blossomed into a global phenomenon. We'll examine how the genre has evolved, the key artists who have shaped its landscape, and the innovative ways in which they've blended different musical influences to create something truly unique. You'll discover that Lo-fi isn't just a passing trend but a complex, multi-faceted genre that continues to grow and change.

One of the most fascinating aspects of lo-fi music is its ability to transcend conventional musical boundaries. While many genres stick to specific structures and themes, Lo-fi thrives on experimentation. Artists often blend elements from a variety of influences, including jazz, hip-hop, and electronic music. This fusion results in a sound that's refreshingly original yet comfortingly familiar.

Beyond the technicalities and history, lo-fi music holds a special place in our cultural landscape. It's more than just background music for studying or relaxing—it's a form of artistic expression that taps into universal human experiences and emotions. It reminds us that beauty can be found in the raw and unfiltered, in the moments of quiet introspection, and in the simple joy of being present. In the digital age, where everything seems to move at breakneck speed, Lo-fi provides a much-needed pause.

But why should we care about understanding lo-fi music? Why should this genre demand our attention in a world saturated with countless other musical styles? The answer lies in Lo-fi's profound impact on listeners and its growing influence on contemporary culture. By exploring the roots of lo-fi music, we gain insights into a lifestyle that values mindfulness, creativity, and emotional connection.

As we journey through the captivating world of lo-fi music, you'll meet the visionary minds who have propelled this genre forward, as well as the pioneering artists who left an indelible mark on the lo-fi landscape.

For adult listeners eager to discover the unique charm of Lo-fi, consider this your guide to a genre that transcends conventional musical boundaries. You'll find yourself captivated by the enchanting allure of imperfect sounds and the emotional depth they bring. We encourage you to explore the subtleties of lo-fi music with an open mind, and you'll uncover a world rich in texture, emotion, and history.

So, let's discover the many layers and dimensions of lo-fi music together. Along the way, you'll not only expand your musical horizons but also gain a newfound appreciation for the art of imperfection. After all, in the world of Lo-fi, it's the unpolished gem that truly shines.

Chapter 1

Understanding Lo-fi Music

When you dive into the world of lo-fi music, one of the first things you'll notice is how wonderfully raw and unpolished it all sounds. It's a far cry from the ultra-clean, meticulously produced tracks that dominate the mainstream music scene, and that's also a big part of what makes Lo-fi so special.

Instead of striving for technical perfection, lo-fi artists embrace the little imperfections that come with their humble, homemade setups. It could be the faint hiss of an old cassette tape or the slightly out-of-tune notes from a battered keyboard.

It's those imperfections that give the music such an intimate, nostalgic quality, which feels wonderfully human and authentic.

It's not just the technical aspects that set Lo-fi apart—the genre's inherent simplicity is a big part of the appeal, too. Rather than packing their songs with layers of complexity, lo-fi artists tend to keep things stripped-back and minimalist, letting the melodies and rhythms shine through.

Ultimately, what draws so many listeners to lo-fi music is its ability to tap into something primal and emotional. It's a listening experience that's grounded, intimate, and soulful.

Definition and Characteristics of Lo-fi Music

To truly appreciate lo-fi music, you need to understand its core elements, such as the lo-fi aesthetic and production, which is characterized by a raw, unpolished sound. This unique quality often includes imperfections like background noise, tape hiss, or even misplayed notes. Far from being seen as flaws, these elements add to the charm and authenticity of the genre. Lo-fi music embraces these "errors" to create a nostalgic and intimate listening experience. These rough edges make the music feel more human, allowing listeners to connect on a deeper emotional level.

Lo-fi music is a departure from the overproduced tracks that dominate mainstream music. In lo-fi, the focus is not on achieving sonic perfection but on conveying warmth and relatability. This takes us back to the roots of home recordings, where musicians had limited resources and had to make do with what they had. The result is a genre that feels genuine and accessible, much like a handwritten letter in an age of digital communication.

The lo-fi production style encourages creativity. Artists are free to experiment without worrying about meeting industry standards. This freedom fosters innovation, giving rise to unique sounds and styles within the genre.

Sampling is another key aspect of lo-fi music. It involves repurposing snippets of existing records—be it old jazz records, nature sounds, or even movie dialogues. This technique allows artists to create richly layered tracks that resonate with layers of meaning.

Even though they're using bits from other places, they're making something completely new. It's like making a collage with sounds instead of pictures.

Sampling in Lo-fi isn't just about borrowing; it's about reimagining.

Artists take familiar sounds and give them a fresh context, transforming them into something that fits seamlessly into the laid-back vibe of the genre. This process often leads to moments of serendipity, where unexpected combinations produce surprisingly captivating results.

The use of sampling also democratizes music production. With today's technology, anyone can access vast libraries of sounds and manipulate them using basic software. As a result, the style is growing fast and becoming more varied.

Finally, lo-fi music is all about creating a chill vibe. It's known for being relaxing and calm, perfect for when you're studying, working, or just wanting to unwind. The slow beats and soft melodies will help you feel peaceful.

Many lo-fi tracks include soothing sounds like rain or ocean waves, which can make you feel like you're in a quiet, peaceful place. The steady rhythm can be almost hypnotic, helping you focus or de-stress.

Lo-fi isn't just about the sound, though. It often comes with calming visuals, like animations of cozy rooms or beautiful scenery. This combination of sound and image creates a little oasis of calm in your day.

What makes Lo-fi really interesting is how it mixes different types of music. It borrows from hip-hop, jazz, and electronic music, creating something new and exciting. Artists use both old-school instruments and modern tech to create their tracks, which keeps the style fresh and appealing to lots of different people.

The Cultural Significance of Lo-fi Music

Lo-fi music, with its characteristic low-fidelity sound and nostalgic vibes, has a rich cultural history that shapes its modern persona. This genre traces its origins to the countercultural roots of the DIY and underground music movements. In the 1980s, indie rock bands such as The Mountain Goats and Beck epitomized the essence of DIY culture by producing music with whatever equipment they had on hand, welcoming imperfections as part of their artistic expression.

As recording gear became more affordable, music-making became available to anyone with a computer and basic equipment. This spirit of innovation opened the doors to all kinds of new sounds in Lo-fi.

The rise of internet culture has played an important role in propelling lo-fi music to unprecedented heights. Online communities on platforms like Reddit, YouTube, and SoundCloud have become hubs for sharing and discovering new lo-fi tracks. Channels like ChilledCow and College Music stream lo-fi playlists 24/7, creating virtual spaces where listeners can connect and engage with the genre.

The lo-fi community is like a big, supportive family, and the music style has grown by letting artists share their work directly with fans. Instead of needing to be on TV or radio to get noticed, lo-fi artists can share their music online and find people who love it.

Internet algorithms also contribute significantly to the genre's popularity. Playlists and recommendation engines help listeners discover lo-fi music they might not have discovered otherwise.

Thanks to the internet, lo-fi music can reach audiences worldwide. It's like having a universal language that everyone can understand and enjoy, no matter where they're from or what culture they're part of.

Lo-fi music is like a friendly neighbor that everyone likes, no matter where they're from. Since it doesn't have words, anyone can enjoy it without worrying about language barriers. People all over the world use Lo-fi as background music while they study, work, or just relax.

For the people making Lo-fi, it's a chance to be creative without worrying about making hit songs. They can play around with different sounds and make music that feels personal to them.

For listeners, Lo-fi is like a cozy blanket for their ears. Its gentle, repeating beats can help you focus when you're studying or working. It's also great for relaxing after a stressful day. Many people find that Lo-fi helps them feel calm and peaceful in their busy lives.

So, whether you're making it or listening to it, lo-fi music has a special way of making people feel good and connected, no matter where they are in the world.

Lo-fi vs. Other Music Genres

When contrasting the production techniques of lo-fi music with mainstream genres like pop or rock, the approach to sound quality and recording environments is very different. Mainstream pop and rock often rely on high-end studios, advanced technology, and meticulous editing to create a polished, flawless sound. In contrast, lo-fi music embraces a DIY ethos where music is recorded in home setups using basic equipment. This results in a raw, unpolished sound that captures background noises and imperfections, which are considered part of its charm rather than flaws to be corrected.

Mainstream productions usually prioritize clarity, balance, and frequency range, aiming for pristine audio perfect for radio play and streaming. Producers spend hours refining every detail, ensuring each instrument and vocal track is crisply defined and perfectly mixed. On the other hand, lo-fi producers often intentionally incorporate elements like tape hiss, vinyl crackles, and environmental sounds into their tracks. These "imperfections" create a cozy, intimate atmosphere, which can evoke feelings of nostalgia and authenticity for listeners (Neal, A., 2022).

The tools and techniques used also differ significantly. Mainstream genres use the latest software and hardware to achieve sophisticated effects and dynamic ranges. In contrast, lo-fi artists might use outdated or simple gear, including old cassette recorders or lo-fi samplers, and focus on creating loops and beats that have a laid-back, dreamy quality. This shapes the genre's unique auditory aesthetic and also reflects a more accessible, egalitarian approach to music production where anyone with a computer and some creativity can participate.

Aesthetic choices in lo-fi music further set it apart from mainstream genres by prioritizing simplicity and embracing imperfections. While mainstream music often strives for perfection through complex arrangements and highly produced tracks, lo-fi music opts for minimalistic compositions and lo-fi aesthetics. This can include deliberately adding "errors" like off-tune notes or timing irregularities to create a sense of organic, human warmth. These choices make the music feel more relatable and less manufactured, contributing to its soothing, calming effect.

The visual and thematic elements associated with lo-fi music also reflect this preference for simplicity. Album covers and music videos often feature nostalgic, low-fi animations or illustrations that align with the music's vibe. This creates a holistic experience where both audio and visual components work together to establish a relaxed, introspective mood. Lo-fi music is more about creating a calm atmosphere than catchy tunes. Unlike loud, flashy pop songs, Lo-fi aims to surround you with a cozy feeling. It's like a quiet night in versus a big party—Lo-fi wants to help you relax, while mainstream music often tries to get you excited.

Lo-fi music often carries a distinct warmth, and its rough edges make it feel like a companion. This authenticity resonates deeply with listeners seeking music that feels genuine and personal. The genre's simplicity and imperfections become strengths, fostering a unique connection between the artist and listener.

Lo-fi music often taps into deep emotional connections, evoking feelings of nostalgia and introspection. The music is emotionally appealing because of its warm, mellow tones, repetitive rhythms, and samples that remind listeners of past eras or life's simpler moments. Many describe listening to Lo-fi music as a comforting experience that feels like revisiting cherished memories.

Lo-fi music has a special way of connecting with listeners on an emotional level. It's often played in the background during intimate moments—when you're studying, relaxing, or reflecting late at night. As you engage with the music during these personal times, it becomes part of your experiences, taking on a deeper, more sentimental meaning.

The nostalgic elements of Lo-fi, like the crackly vinyl sounds and imperfect loops, transport you back in time. It's a refreshing contrast to the constant push for newness and innovation in mainstream music. Lo-fi offers a comforting escape, allowing you to pause and reflect amidst the fast pace of modern life.

The audience can engage in online platforms, especially YouTube and Spotify. Listeners often gather in live-stream chats, sharing their thoughts, feelings, and even personal stories while tuning in to lo-fi beats. This communal aspect creates a shared experience, fostering connections among listeners worldwide.

The rise of continuous lo-fi streams, like the iconic Lo-fi Girl (formerly ChilledCow) channel on YouTube, has become hubs for community interaction. These streams run 24/7, providing a constant backdrop for studying, working, or relaxing, and include chatrooms where fans can discuss the music, share tips, or simply enjoy the presence of others. This real-time interaction builds a sense of belonging and turns passive listening into an active social experience. Fans often feel they are part of a movement or culture rather than just consumers of music (Neal, A., 2022).

The Growing Popularity of Lo-fi Music

Lo-fi music, often characterized by its mellow beats and relaxed ambiance, has significantly risen in prominence over recent years. Online platforms like YouTube and Spotify have played a crucial role in bringing lo-fi music to the mainstream. YouTube channels such as "ChilledCow" and "Lo-fi hip hop radio- beats to relax/study" have millions of subscribers tuning in daily for steady streams of lo-fi music, creating a dedicated audience base (Amable, J., 2019). These platforms provide easy access for listeners worldwide, allowing the genre to reach a broader audience than ever before.

Spotify, with its curated playlists like "Lo-Fi Beats," has significantly contributed to the widespread appeal of lo-fi music. By including lo-fi tracks in these popular collections, Spotify has introduced countless users to the unique sounds of lo-fi music.

The algorithm-driven recommendations on Spotify and YouTube further ensure that once users engage with lo-fi music, they are likely to continue discovering new artists and tracks within the genre. This accessibility and discoverability have been instrumental in establishing lo-fi music's place in contemporary music culture.

Many lo-fi music streams on YouTube include relaxing videos or pictures, such as cute cartoons or peaceful scenes. It's like having a mini-movie playing while you listen to the music—it's almost like having a cozy, animated screensaver that matches the mood of the music. This extra touch makes the whole experience more enjoyable and draws in folks who like how it looks as much as how it sounds.

This friendly back-and-forth helps everyone feel more connected. It's like being part of a large lo-fi music family. Fans get to know the artists better, and artists learn what their listeners like. This teamwork between creators and fans helps keep lo-fi music fresh and exciting.

Key Takeaways

- The lo-fi aesthetic is a statement against polished mainstream tracks.
- It conveys warmth and relatability through simplicity.
- Sampling is significant in Lo-fi, allowing existing sounds to be creatively reimagined.
- Lo-fi democratizes music production, making it accessible to many.
- The genre creates a relaxing atmosphere, ideal for studying or unwinding.
- Lo-fi culture includes soothing visuals, enhancing the overall experience.
- It blends genres like hip-hop, jazz, and electronic music.
- Lo-fi appeals to a wide audience due to its versatility.
- It's a cultural movement rooted in DIY spirit.
- Internet platforms like YouTube and Spotify have facilitated its growth.
- Lo-fi connects with listeners through authenticity and emotional resonance.
- The genre's future evolution is a topic of interest.

- Lo-fi encourages appreciation of imperfections and simplicity.
- It serves as a reminder to slow down and enjoy the present moment.

Chapter 2

Origins and Early Influences of Lo-fi Music

The origins of lo-fi music are a fascinating story. It all starts with this intersection of technology and creativity that really shaped the genre's one-of-a-kind sound. Musicians didn't always have access to all the sleek, high-tech recording gear that we take for granted these days. Instead, they had to be more inventive with the tools they had on hand.

That limitation ended up being a blessing in disguise. Rather than trying to chase after the polished perfection of mainstream music, these early Lo-fi pioneers embraced the inherent imperfections of their budget-friendly setups. The tape hiss, the slight warble, the occasionally sour notes—they recognized that these so-called "flaws" were actually what gave the music its undeniable charm and character.

It was like they were saying, "Hey, we may not have the fanciest gear, but that's not gonna stop us from making something truly special." By harnessing the unique qualities of their lo-fi equipment, they were able to craft a sonic signature that was unlike anything else out there.

Now, the origins of Lo-fi stretch back to all kinds of musical movements—whether it was the Lo-fi rock of the 1980s, the homemade sounds of the DIY punk scene, or the sampling explorations of early hip-hop. No matter where it came from, the through line was always this idea of prioritizing authenticity and creative expression over technical polish.

As recording technology continued to evolve, lo-fi artists just found new and inventive ways to maintain that rawness and imperfection. They might sample crackly old vinyl, manipulate cassette tapes, or even build their own custom gear—whatever it took to keep that irreplaceable human touch in the music.

So, in many ways, the origins of Lo-fi are a testament to the power of creativity and ingenuity. These musicians didn't let the limitations of their equipment hold them back. Instead, they turned those supposed constraints into opportunities for exploration and innovation.

Early Developments in Recording Technology

Technological advancements have heavily influenced the evolution of lo-fi music, starting with the increasing availability of portable recording devices. Before these devices became available, artists were bound to traditional studio settings to produce their music. Portable recorders allowed musicians to capture sound in various environments, from bedrooms to parks. This freedom enabled the raw and unpolished quality of recordings that became a hallmark of the Lo-fi genre. Artists began to appreciate the beauty of imperfections, such as background noise and ambient sounds, that these devices captured.

One prominent example of this shift is how street musicians or amateur bands could now record their performances without needing an expensive studio setup. The very essence of Lo-fi—a laid-back, nostalgic vibe—was born from these unrefined recordings. Traditional studios, with their pristine audio quality and controlled environments, couldn't replicate the organic feel that portable recorders introduced to the music.

As portable recording technology advanced, it led to a surge in home-based music production. Musicians who were previously unable to afford studio time now had the tools to create and distribute their songs independently.

Magnetic Tape TecBhnology

Magnetic tape technology brought another layer of depth to the growth of lo-fi music. This technology allowed artists to experiment with manipulating tape speed, producing effects that added character to their recordings. By slowing down or speeding up tapes, musicians could create unique sonic textures that were both intriguing and aesthetically pleasing.

The magnetic tape also gave the recordings warmth and texture. The intimate and personal nature of the music also draws listeners into the artist's world. The use of magnetic tape allowed for creative sound layering, making it possible to build complex, rich soundscapes with relatively simple equipment.

Magnetic tape sets the tone for entire albums and projects within the Lo-fi genre. This analog approach fostered a deeper connection between the artist and their craft, further endearing lo-fi music to its audience.

Influence of Analog Sound and Imperfections

Analog equipment imparts a unique warmth and character to lo-fi music, setting it apart from other genres. Unlike digital recordings, which strive for pristine sound quality, analog devices such as tape recorders and vinyl turntables introduce subtle imperfections like tape hiss and vinyl crackle. These elements add a layer of texture that many listeners find appealing. The physical properties of analog recordings create a sense of depth and dimension, producing a richer auditory experience.

Tape hiss and vinyl crackle have become synonymous with the lo-fi aesthetic. When you listen to a lo-fi track, the presence of these imperfections can transport you to an earlier, simpler time. For instance, the crackle of a vinyl record can evoke memories of sitting in a cozy room, enveloped by the warmth of nostalgic musical moments. This connection to the past gives lo-fi music its distinct charm.

The imperfections in analog recordings serve as a counterpoint to the sterile perfection of modern digital audio. They embrace the inevitability of flaws and, in doing so, create a more organic listening experience. Such characteristics are not merely tolerated but celebrated within the lo-fi community, making these tracks feel more human and less mechanical.

Lo-fi artists see these imperfections as integral to their craft rather than defects to be removed. In today's music industry, high-fidelity standards often demand polish and precision, but lo-fi artists consciously reject this notion. By embracing the raw, unfiltered sounds produced by analog equipment, they highlight the authenticity and genuineness of their work.

Authenticity is a key value for many lo-fi musicians who aim to capture real, unvarnished moments. This approach stands in stark contrast to mainstream music, where extensive editing usually takes place. A single imperfect recording can capture a unique atmosphere or emotion that would be lost in a more polished production. This willingness to accept and even celebrate mistakes sets lo-fi music apart from other genres.

This emphasis on imperfections also underscores a broader departure from conventional norms. In a world obsessed with flawless performance, lo-fi music serves as a reminder that beauty can be found in imperfection. It challenges listeners to appreciate the raw and the unrefined, offering a refreshing alternative to the highly produced tracks dominating the charts.

The emotional depth achieved through imperfect recordings can create a profound sense of intimacy and vulnerability. Listening to a lo-fi track can feel like sharing a personal moment with the artist, where each flaw and imperfection contributes to the storytelling. This closeness allows listeners to form a deeper emotional connection with the music.

Lo-fi tracks often evoke feelings of nostalgia and melancholy, heightened by their imperfect nature. When an artist intentionally incorporates elements like background noise or off-kilter rhythms, they add layers of emotional complexity to their work. These imperfections invite listeners to lean in and engage more deeply with the music, fostering a sense of empathy and understanding.

By creating an emotionally rich tapestry, lo-fi music becomes more than just sound—it becomes an experience. The minor flaws and imperfections humanize the music, making it relatable and accessible. This emotional resonance helps distinguish Lo-fi from more polished genres, offering a unique listening experience that touches the heart.

Flaws in analog recordings significantly contribute to the nostalgic and humanized quality of lo-fi compositions. Elements like the tape hiss and vinyl crackle are not just background noise; they act as auditory cues that evoke a bygone era. These imperfections lend a sense of history to the tracks, connecting contemporary listeners with older forms of media and musical expression.

Key Musical Influences and Genres

Lo-fi music draws heavily from jazz and hip-hop traditions, creating a unique fusion that sets it apart. The genre often incorporates sampled jazz melodies, which bring a sense of familiarity and warmth. These melodies are typically paired with laid-back beats commonly used in hip-hop, causing listeners to sway gently to the rhythm. This juxtaposition of smooth jazz tones and rhythmic hip-hop elements allows lo-fi tracks to feel both nostalgic and contemporary.

Jazz and Hip-Hop

The influence of jazz and hip-hop can be traced back to the way lo-fi artists use improvisation and rhythmic patterns. Jazz is known for its spontaneous solos and complex chord progressions, which lo-fi producers replicate by sampling classic jazz records. Meanwhile, hip-hop's foundation in beat-making and layering creates a rhythmic backbone essential to Lo-fi music. Artists like Nujabes and J Dilla have expertly blended these genres, demonstrating the seamless integration of jazz aesthetics into hip-hop frameworks.

This fusion reflects a blend of improvisation and rhythmic elements, making each lo-fi track feel fresh yet rooted in tradition. The use of vinyl crackle and tape hiss adds an extra layer of authenticity, evoking a sense of listening to old records. These subtle imperfections are cherished rather than polished away, emphasizing the genre's appreciation for raw, unfiltered sounds. Lo-fi music ultimately becomes a canvas where the past and present coalesce, creating a timeless auditory experience.

Ambient Music and Electronic Experimentation

Ambient music and electronic experimentation play significant roles in shaping Lo-fi soundscapes. Synthesizers, ambient textures, and lo-fi effects are commonly used to create dreamy and immersive atmospheres. These elements help add depth and dimension to lo-fi tracks. By incorporating ambient sounds, Lo-fi music transcends traditional genre boundaries.

Electronic experimentation enhances the introspective and immersive nature of Lo-fi music. Producers often manipulate synthesizer patches and ambient sounds to craft ethereal and meditative tracks. This artistic approach encourages listeners to get lost in the layers of sound, making each listening session a personal journey. Legendary ambient artists like Brian Eno have inspired many lo-fi musicians to explore these sonic territories, resulting in a rich tapestry of influences within the genre.

These ambient and electronic elements contribute to the distinct character of Lo-fi music, setting it apart from other genres. The gentle hum of a synthesizer or the echo of a distant reverb can evoke emotions and memories, creating a deeply personal connection with the listener. This atmospheric quality makes lo-fi perfect for study sessions, relaxation, or simply enjoying a quiet moment. Through ambient influences, Lo-fi music encourages a peaceful environment for reflection.

Indie Music

Indie music's DIY spirit has also left a significant mark on lo-fi productions. The ethos of doing it yourself encourages creativity and authenticity, which are core values in the Lo-fi community. Many lo-fi artists prefer to work independently, recording in home studios and using everyday objects as instruments. This hands-on approach allows for greater artistic freedom and personal expression, resulting in music that feels genuine and heartfelt.

DIY Approach

DIY approaches encourage innovation and genre-blurring in lo-fi compositions. By stepping outside the confines of traditional music production, lo-fi artists can blend various influences and create something entirely new. This innovative mindset leads to tracks that are not easily categorized but are unmistakably Lo-fi. The willingness to embrace imperfection and experiment with different sounds ensures that the genre remains dynamic and evolving, constantly pushing creative boundaries.

Pioneers of the Lo-fi Movement

The pioneers of Lo-fi music are responsible for creating the genre's unique sound. Nujabes stands out among these trailblazers. Known for his innovative blend of jazz samples and lo-fi production techniques, Nujabes brought a fresh dimension to hip-hop. His work is often characterized by smooth, soulful beats layered with intricate jazz melodies, creating an atmospheric and mellow vibe that resonates deeply with listeners. By intertwining jazz elements with hip-hop rhythms, Nujabes not only created a new auditory experience but also laid the groundwork for future producers to explore similar fusions.

Najubes

Nujabes was a true visionary in the world of Lo-fi music, and his influence can still be felt across the genre today. What set him apart was his revolutionary approach to production—he had a way of utilizing analog equipment and sampling that gave his tracks a warm, nostalgic quality unlike anything else out there.

While a lot of producers at the time were chasing that super clean, high-fidelity sound, Nujabes embraced a much more imperfect, lo-fi aesthetic. He actually appreciated the little flaws and imperfections that came with his production methods, like the natural tape hiss or the crackle of vinyl. Rather than trying to smooth everything out, Nujabes leaned into those elements, allowing them to imbue his music with a sense of authenticity and intimacy.

The result was a sound that felt so much more human and relatable than the ultra-polished stuff. There was this palpable warmth and soul to Nujabes' productions that you couldn't replicate with pristine digital recordings. It was like you were getting a direct window into his creative process—the little quirks and idiosyncrasies that made each track feel alive and lived-in.

Nujabes' pioneering spirit and innovative techniques have had a huge impact on the Lo-fi scene as a whole. Even today, you can hear his influence woven into the work of countless contemporary lo-fi artists. They're taking inspiration from his blending of genres, his embrace of raw soundscapes, and his willingness to let imperfections shine. It's a testament to the timeless quality of Nujabes' vision.

Whether it's through direct sampling of his work or a more general stylistic homage, Nujabes' legacy continues to reverberate throughout the Lo-fi community. His music can be found on countless playlists, introducing new listeners to that signature warm, nostalgic sound. And for Lo-fi fans, Nujabes' productions serve as a touchstone—a reminder of the genre's roots and the power of authenticity in music.

Ultimately, what made Nujabes such an important figure was his unwavering commitment to his own artistic vision. He didn't care about chasing trends or conforming to industry standards. Instead, he forged his own path, using analog gear and sampling in ways that felt true to his unique sensibilities. And in doing so, he didn't just create a body of work that was hugely influential—he also left an indelible mark on the very fabric of Lo-fi music itself. Nujabes has made an undeniable and enduring impact on the genre.

DJ Shadow

DJ Shadow is a true trailblazer in the world of music production. He's known for his innovative and experimental use of sampling, which has revolutionized the way producers approach creating new tracks.

One of DJ Shadow's most celebrated works is his album, *Endtroducing.....*, which is often hailed as a masterpiece of sample-based production. Instead of just relying on the usual sources, he dug deep into his collection of obscure records to find all sorts of interesting sounds and snippets. Then, he carefully wove these samples together into dense, collage-like tracks that defied traditional genre boundaries.

This approach was a game-changer. Rather than sticking to a single style or sound, DJ Shadow proved that you could create something completely unique and genre-blending by repurposing existing material. Each sample he used became a building block in a larger, more textured musical landscape. The end result was music that was rich in depth, emotion, and meaning.

What made DJ Shadow's work so special was the way he elevated sampling from a simple technique into an art form. He showed that by thoughtfully selecting and manipulating samples, producers could imbue their tracks with layers of complexity and creativity, opening up a whole new world of musical possibilities.

DJ Shadow's influence can be felt far and wide, even today. His pioneering work has paved the way for a new generation of lo-fi artists to experiment with sampling in their own compositions. Many of them drawing direct inspiration from DJ Shadow's unorthodox approach, using diverse sounds and unconventional structures to craft music that's distinctly their own.

In a way, DJ Shadow's legacy is a testament to the power of sampling.

He proved that by repurposing existing material, you can create something entirely new and meaningful. His work serves as a shining example of how creativity can flourish when you're willing to think outside the box and push the boundaries of what's possible in music production.

So, the next time you hear a DJ Shadow track or the work of an artist inspired by his methods, take a moment to appreciate the rich history and innovation behind it all. It's a reminder that sampling isn't just a tool—it's a pathway to boundless musical expression.

J Dilla

J Dilla's impact on the Lo-fi music scene can't be overstated. As one of the genre's pioneering figures, he brought a distinct approach to beat-making that has left an indelible mark.

Unlike some producers who prized technical perfection above all else, J Dilla embraced a much more raw, homegrown aesthetic. He was known for using lo-fi, DIY production methods that gave his tracks an organically imperfect quality. Rather than coming across as sloppy or unfinished, this lo-fi sound was integral to the deep emotional resonance of his music.

A big part of J Dilla's signature style came from his unconventional use of equipment. Instead of relying on pristine digital tools, he would often manipulate analog gear like tape decks to achieve those delightfully imperfect textures. Maybe it was a subtle flutter in the playback or some unexpected warble—little quirks that added so much character and humanity to the sound.

For J Dilla, these kinds of imperfections weren't flaws to be smoothed over; they were an essential part of the creative process. He understood that beauty often lies in the rough edges, the unintended moments that give the music a sense of life and feeling. This was a philosophy that stood in stark contrast to the clinical precision of manydigital productions at the time.

This willingness to prioritize emotional resonance over technical perfection was hugely influential, both for J Dilla's contemporaries and the next generation of lo-fi artists—as his work showcased that onedidn't need flawless, studio-quality sound to make music that deeply connects with people. Sometimes, the most powerful artistic statements come from embracing the imperfect, the homemade, the unpolished.

Today, you can hear J Dilla's imprint all over the Lo-fi scene. Many current producers are taking inspiration from his methods, experimenting with lo-fi gear and analog quirks to craft beats that feel organic and alive. They're striving to capture that same raw, soulful vibe that defined J Dilla's music—the sense that you're getting an intimate, unvarnished glimpse into the artist's creative process.

In a way, J Dilla's legacy stands as a powerful rejoinder to the notion that perfection is the key to great music. His work showed that sometimes, the most meaningful and affecting tracks are the ones that feel a little rough around the edges—the ones that let you hear the artist's hand at work. This lesson has reverberated throughout the Lo-fi scene, inspiring a new generation of producers to embrace their own flaws and idiosyncrasies.

Ultimately, J Dilla's impact goes beyond just his own discography. He helped redefine the very idea of what Lo-fi music could be, shifting the focus away from technical prowess and towards a more emotive, human-centric approach. His pioneering spirit lives on in the work of countless artists who continue to push the boundaries of the genre, using lo-fi production as a means of achieving deeper artistic expression. In that sense, J Dilla's legacy is one of timeless, enduring inspiration.

Key Takeaways

- The rise of portable recording technology was a game-changer for Lo-fi music as artists could now capture raw, authentic sounds anywhere—bedrooms, parks, etc.
- Imperfections like background noise and ambient sounds were now embraced.
- Analog equipment like magnetic tape added warmth and texture to the recordings.
- These elements created a more intimate, personal connection between the artist and the listener.
- Affordable home recording gear democratized music production, sparking a grassroots movement.
- Lo-fi artists focused on genuine expression over flawless sound quality.
- Lo-fi blended diverse genres like jazz, hip-hop, and ambient to create introspective soundscapes.
- Pioneering Lo-fi artists like Nujabes, DJ Shadow, and J Dilla inspired generations that followed.
- Lo-fis' evolution reflects broader cultural and technological shifts, empowering more voices to be heard.
- Lo-fi encourages appreciating the beauty in imperfection and connecting with raw, genuine expression.

Chapter 3

The Evolution of Lofi Music

Although lo-fi music has evolved in fascinating ways over the years, at its core is that raw, homespun charm that comes from working with humble, analog equipment. Back in the day, a lot of these early lo-fi artists didn't have access to fancy, high-tech recording studios. Instead, they were making their music on stuff like old cassette tape recorders and four-track machines—the kind of gear that wasn't exactly known for its pristine sound quality.

But you know what? That's exactly what gave Lo-fi its distinctive character and appeal. Rather than trying to smooth out every imperfection, these pioneering producers actually embraced the quirks and flaws that came with their budget-friendly setups. The tape hiss, the distortion, the little glitches and warbles—it all became an integral part of the sonic texture, imbuing the music with a sense of authenticity and emotional resonance that you just can't fake.

When you listen to those early lo-fi tracks, you can almost feel the presence of the artist in the room with you. There's a tangible human element to the sound that goes beyond just the melodies and rhythms. It's like you're getting a direct window into their creative process.

As technology has evolved, lo-fi producers have started incorporating more sophisticated digital tools and techniques into their workflow. However, even as the sound has become more polished and refined, that core analog essence has endured. Whether they're sampling vintage vinyl, manipulating tape loops, or just creatively employing modern gear to achieve a vintage vibe, these artists are always finding ways to preserve that homemade, handcrafted quality that defines the genre.

So, as Lo-fi continues to evolve and grow, that foundational analog spirit will always be there, shaping the music and inspiring new generations of producers to push the boundaries of what's possible.

Transition from Analog to Digital

The roots of lo-fi music lie firmly in analog equipment, which played a vital role in shaping the raw, distinctive sound that defines early lo-fi tracks. Musicians initially used inexpensive, often second-hand recording devices, such as cassette tape recorders and four-track machines. These tools were accessible to independent artists who operated outside traditional studio environments. The analog realm introduced natural imperfections like tape hiss, warble, and distortion, contributing to the unique auditory texture that many enthusiasts cherish.

Analog Limitations

When you look at the origins of lo-fi music, it's fascinating to see how those early artists embraced the limitations of analog recording equipment. Back then, they didn't have access to the pristine, high-tech digital tools that producers use today; instead of seeing that as a problem, they flipped it on its head and turned those constraints into creative strengths.

Take the quality of the recordings, for example. With analog gear, you'd often end up with things like a hiss, crackle, and other little imperfections that would creep into the final sound—and in the hands of a less adventurous artist, that might have been seen as a flaw to be eliminated. But lo-fi pioneers recognized the charm and authenticity that those analog quirks could bring to the music.

Instead of trying to clean everything up, they embraced those gritty, lo-fi textures. The faulty mic setups, the ambient noise in the room—all of that stuff contributed to a raw, energetic vibe that felt so much more genuine and emotionally resonant than the glossy, polished productions that dominated the mainstream at the time.

It's similar to how a painting done with thick, expressive brushstrokes can feel so much more alive and human than a hyper-realistic digital illustration. There's an inherent charm and authenticity to the imperfections, the little flaws that reveal the artist's hand at work, which was what these early lo-fi artists were tapping into.

It wasn't just about the sound quality—the physical process of working with analog gear also lent itself to a more personal, hands-on approach to production. Think about the way you can physically manipulate a tape reel, bending and warping the sound in unique ways. That tactile interaction allowed artists to imbue each recording with their own distinct touch and personality.

Compared to the pristine, clinical nature of digital production, analog felt so much more alive and human. Every hiss, every pop, every bit of ambient noise contributed to a sense of atmosphere and spontaneity that was incredibly alluring. And for listeners who craved that earnest, unvarnished musical experience, Lo-fi's analog charm was exactly what they were looking for.

Of course, these days, lo-fi artists have access to all kinds of digital tools and software. But you can still hear the influence of those early analog pioneers in the music. The embrace of imperfection and the focus on raw emotion and energy are all part of what gives Lo-fi its distinctive character.

The Shift to Digital

As technology progressed, the shift from analog to digital dramatically changed lo-fi music production. Digital audio workstations (DAWs) emerged, revolutionizing the way music was created and recorded. DAWs provided tools that made recording, editing, and mixing far more efficient and versatile compared to their analog counterparts. This shift not only streamlined the process but also made it significantly more accessible to a broader range of artists.

Digital technology has made music production easier by eliminating barriers related to cost and technical expertise. With a computer and affordable software, aspiring musicians can now produce professional-quality tracks from their bedrooms. This accessibility led to an explosion of creativity within the lo-fi community. Artists began experimenting with various sounds and production techniques that were previously out of reach, expanding the boundaries of what Lo-fi music could be.

DAWs also allowed for detailed manipulation of sound, enabling producers to achieve both polished and intentionally degraded audio qualities. Tools like virtual tape machines and effects plug-ins emulated analog imperfections, blending them seamlessly with modern precision. This technological flexibility encouraged innovation and experimentation, fostering the development of new styles within the Lo-fi genre.

Hybrid Approach

The hybrid approach of combining analog warmth with digital precision has opened exciting creative possibilities in modern lo-fi production. Artists now have the best of both worlds: the nostalgic texture of analog and the limitless capabilities of digital. By integrating vintage gear with contemporary software, producers can craft distinctive soundscapes that contrast yet complement each other, creating rich, multi-layered compositions.

Some artists might record guitar parts using analog pedals and amplifiers before transferring the recordings into a DAW for further manipulation and enhancement. This method allows them to retain the organic feel of analog sound while utilizing digital tools to refine the mix. Such practices highlight the versatility and depth achievable in lo-fi music today, bridging the gap between past and present technologies.

There are plenty of examples of hybrid approaches in the current Lo-fi scene. Musicians like Knxwledge and Ta-ku adeptly blend crunchy, vinyl-sampled beats with precise digital production, crafting tracks that feel timeless yet cutting-edge. These hybrid techniques not only preserve the genre's original charm but also enable continuous evolution, ensuring Lo-fi music remains fresh and relevant in an ever-changing musical landscape.

Impact of Internet and Streaming Platforms

The internet has completely transformed the world of lo-fi music, opening up amazing opportunities for artists and fans alike.

One of the biggest game-changers has been the rise of online communities. Places like Reddit, Discord, and YouTube have become hubs where lo-fi fans can gather, share their favorite tracks, and connect with the artists they love. It's this sense of community that makes the genre so special—everyone feels like they're part of something bigger.

These virtual spaces allow for instant feedback and collaboration. Aspiring lo-fi musicians can get constructive critiques from their peers, find potential collaborators, and even discover seasoned veterans who are willing to offer advice and guidance. It's like having a built-in support system to help you grow as an artist.

These online communities span the globe. Lo-fi fans and producers from all different backgrounds can come together, sharing their unique cultural perspectives and musical influences. This cross-pollination of ideas is what keeps the genre feeling fresh and innovative.

Streaming platforms have also had a huge impact on how lo-fi music is discovered and consumed. Curated playlists and personalized recommendations on Spotify and other services have become essential discovery tools. Getting featured on one of those playlists can be a total game-changer for an artist, exposing their work to tons of new listeners overnight.

But it's a double-edged sword—with so much lo-fi music out there, artists have to work harder than ever to stand out. The competition is fierce, and you've got to constantly evolve your sound and upping your production value to stay relevant. It's all about finding that perfect balance between creativity and commercial appeal.

That said, the digital landscape also gives lo-fi musicians some incredible opportunities. They can livestream concerts, collaborate with artists from around the world, and even participate in international festivals—all from the comfort of their home studios. The internet has truly made it possible for them to build global fanbases and sustainable careers.

So, while the digital revolution certainly has challenges, its overall impact on lo-fi music has been massively positive. It's opened up new avenues for connection, discovery, and artistic growth. For fans, this means we get to experience this wonderful genre in richer, more diverse ways than ever before.

Shifts in Production Techniques

Over the years, production techniques in lo-fi music have evolved to preserve the genre's nostalgic charm while embracing modern influences. Artists blend traditional analog sounds with contemporary digital effects, creating hybrid tracks that feel both timeless and current. This fusion allows for greater experimentation, enabling producers to push the boundaries of what defines the Lo-fi genre while still honoring its roots.

Experimental Sound Design

Experimental sound design practices have played an important role in pushing the sonic boundaries of lo-fi music. Incorporating field recordings and found sounds has become a popular technique among lo-fi artists, adding layers of texture and atmosphere to their compositions. These unconventional methods allow for a richer auditory experience, where mundane sounds from everyday life—like rain, footsteps, or city noise—become integral parts of the musical narrative.

Field Recordings

Field recordings offer an authentic and immersive quality to lo-fi tracks, often evoking specific emotions or memories in listeners. This approach transforms ordinary environments into unique soundscapes, allowing artists to paint vivid sonic pictures using minimalistic yet impactful elements. By weaving these real-world sounds into their music, lo-fi producers invite listeners on a journey that feels both personal and universal.

The use of found sounds also challenges conventional notions of music production, emphasizing creativity and resourcefulness over technical perfection. "Found sounds" is a term used in lo-fi music to describe the incorporation of unexpected, everyday noises and environmental recordings into musical compositions. This experimental mindset encourages artists to explore new sonic territories, leading to innovative compositions that defy traditional genre boundaries.

Role of Independent Artists

The independent, DIY spirit has always been the driving force behind the lo-fi music scene, and for good reason. It's this unwavering commitment to creative freedom and authenticity that gives the genre its distinctive charm and enduring appeal.

At the core of the Lo-fi ethos is a refusal to play by the traditional rules of the music industry. These artists aren't interested in chasing commercial success or conforming to someone else's idea of what their music should sound like. Instead, they embrace a do-it-yourself mentality, using whatever limited resources they have at their disposal to craft something truly unique and personal.

Take Randall Taylor, who records under the name Amulets, as a prime example. Rather than relying on expensive studio gear, he uses everyday household items like cassette tapes and guitar pedals to create his hauntingly beautiful ambient compositions. The result is an unmistakably homemade sound—it has a warmth and imperfection that you just can't replicate with polished, high-tech productions.

Randall's approach is about more than just the gear he uses. It's about maintaining complete creative control over his artistic vision without having to answer to record labels or industry executives. This freedom allows him to continuously experiment, diving deeper into his own musical exploration without worrying about trends or commercial appeal.

Randall is far from the only lo-fi artist who's carved out this kind of independent path. In fact, the entire scene is teeming with innovators who are pushing the boundaries of what's possible within the genre. Whether they're self-releasing their music on Bandcamp or joining forces with like-minded collectives, these musicians are firmly focused on forging their own unique sounds and artistic identities.

Platforms like Chillhop Music and Inner Ocean Records have played a crucial role in nurturing and elevating this independent spirit. Rather than operating like faceless corporations, these labels function more like close-knit communities of creatives, providing emerging lo-fi artists with the resources, exposure, and collaborative opportunities they need to thrive.

It's this sense of community and mutual support that is truly special about the independent Lo-fi scene. These artists aren't just creating music in isolation—they're actively building networks, sharing knowledge, and inspiring each other to keep exploring new sonic territories. It's a culture of creativity and camaraderie that is essential to the genre's ongoing evolution.

The synergy between lo-fi music and visual art is another area where this independent ethos really shines. By collaborating with animators, filmmakers, and visual artists, lo-fi musicians are able to craft immersive, multi-sensory experiences that transcend the purely auditory realm. This is a testament to the genre's boundless potential for innovation and experimentation.

Ultimately, what makes the independent Lo-fi scene so captivating is the way it prioritizes authenticity, community, and creative freedom over commercial aspirations. These artists aren't chasing fame or fortune—they're driven by a pure, unadulterated love of the craft and a desire to push the boundaries of what's possible within their chosen medium. It's a spirit of innovation that will always be at the heart of Lo-fi music, ensuring that the genre continues to evolve and surprise listeners for years to come.

Key Takeaways

- Lo-fi music started with musicians using inexpensive, imperfect equipment that introduced natural flaws, creating a warm, nostalgic sound.
- The rise of digital audio workstations (DAWs) made music production more accessible, leading to an explosion of creativity and experimentation in the lo-fi community.
- Online communities and streaming platforms have revolutionized the Lo-fi scene, helping artists and fans connect and discover new music.
- DIY lo-fi artists embrace imperfections and creative freedom, constantly innovating and pushing the boundaries of the genre.
- Lo-fi musicians often partner with visual artists, poets, and other creatives to enhance the multimedia experience of their work.
- Lo-fi artists combine elements from diverse genres, such as hip-hop, jazz, electronic, and world music, to create rich and diverse soundscapes.
- While the digital era has provided more opportunities, it has also led to increased competition, making it harder for artists to

stand out.

- Lo-fi music will continue to evolve and transform, adapting to changing technologies and tastes while maintaining its unique blend of old and new and its embrace of imperfections.

Chapter 4

Production Techniques in Lo-fi Music

When it comes to lo-fi music, the production techniques artists use are a big part of what gives the genre its distinctive charm and character. Instead of striving for a super clean, polished sound, lo-fi producers embrace the quirks and imperfections that come from working with vintage gear and old-school sampling methods.

Take those crackles and pops you hear—the kind that comes from playing an old vinyl record. Or the subtle hum of a tape deck as the music spills out. These little analog artifacts aren't flaws to be ironed out; they're an essential part of the lo-fi aesthetic. Producers purposefully weave them into their tracks, using them to create a warm, nostalgic atmosphere that you just can't replicate with pristine digital recordings.

It's not just about throwing some old-sounding samples into the mix. The true magic of lo-fi production lies in how these elements are blended and manipulated to evoke specific emotions and vibes. It's about carefully crafting the rhythmic foundation with looped beats that have this organic, human feel—not the rigidly quantized percussion you'd find in more polished genres.

By embracing imperfections and blending vintage sounds in creative ways, lo-fi producers can craft tracks that feel deeply atmospheric and immersive. The music has a certain mood and ambiance that really resonates on an emotional level, transporting the listener to a specific time and place.

Perhaps it's the wistful melancholy of a track that samples an old jazz record or the tranquil, meditative vibe of a beat that incorporates nature sounds and field recordings. Whatever the specific flavor, the production choices play a huge role in shaping the overall character and impact of the music.

So, when you're listening to Lo-fi, try to tune in not just to the melodies and rhythms but also to the textures and tones that make up the sonic landscape. Pay attention to how those little imperfections and analog flourishes contribute to the atmosphere. It's a big part of what gives the genre its distinctive personality, making it so enchanting to discover and explore.

Use of Sampling and Looping

Sampling and *looping* are foundational techniques in lo-fi music production. These practices give lo-fi tracks their distinctive, nostalgic sound. Producers often scout for unique records and tapes that offer a range of sounds—crackles, pops, and all—that evoke a sense of history and warmth. The imperfections found in these old recordings add character to the music, making each track feel more organic and real.

The charm of vintage samples lies in their authenticity. Using snippets from older records, producers can craft an auditory palette that feels timeless. Many iconic lo-fi tracks use jazz, soul, or even classical music as their base, filtering and tweaking them to fit modern beats and moods. This process can involve days of searching through thrift store bins or online marketplaces for that perfect soundbite that brings a track to life. The vintage elements create a familiar, yet fresh listening experience deeply rooted in musical history.

Incorporating these vintage samples requires skill and creativity. Producers need to isolate the best parts of a record, clean up any unwanted noise while preserving its character, and then blend it seamlessly into their compositions. This balancing act ensures that the music retains its old-world charm while fitting neatly into a contemporary soundscape. The result is music that feels both new and nostalgically comforting, capturing the essence of what makes Lo-fi so compelling.

Loop manipulation is another important aspect of producing lo-fi music. Loops are short, repeating sections of audio that form the backbone of many tracks. The art of manipulating these loops involves stretching, shrinking, and occasionally adding effects to make them more engaging. By playing with the timing and tempo, producers can create grooves that are both hypnotic and relaxing, perfect for background listening or deep-focus sessions.

One common technique is *time-stretching*, where a loop's length is altered without changing its pitch. This method allows producers to match loops of different tempos, ensuring a cohesive flow throughout the track. Another approach is *adding effects* such as reverb or delay to make loops feel more spacious and immersive. These subtle changes can transform simple loops into rich, textured canvases that evoke various emotions in listeners.

Manipulating loops also requires a keen ear for detail. Each adjustment can significantly alter the mood of a track, so producers must tweak their loops carefully. They often experiment with different combinations, layering multiple loops to create complex, evolving soundscapes. The goal is to maintain repetition without becoming monotonous, striking a balance between predictability and surprise.

The creative process of chopping and rearranging samples is essential in crafting lo-fi tracks. *Chopping* involves cutting longer audio segments into smaller pieces, which can then be rearranged to form new patterns. This technique gives producers immense control over their material, allowing them to create intricate, multi-layered compositions from simple building blocks.

Producers often start by identifying the most interesting parts of a sample—perhaps a catchy drum break or a soulful melody. They then slice these segments into manageable chunks, which can be rearranged to produce entirely new phrases. This method enables the creation of unique rhythmic and melodic structures that wouldn't be possible using unaltered samples alone.

Once chopped, these samples can be further manipulated. *Pitch-shifting*, adding effects, or even *reversing* specific segments can introduce unexpected twists and turns in a track. The challenge lies in making these disparate elements cohere into a unified piece of music. Successful chopping and *rearranging* require a fine balance between technical skill and artistic intuition, resulting in lo-fi tracks that feel both innovative and familiar.

Layering different samples to add texture and depth is another hallmark of lo-fi music production. This technique involves stacking multiple audio tracks on top of each other, each contributing its unique character to the overall sound. Effective layering can make a track sound fuller and richer, creating a more immersive listening experience.

Each layer serves a specific purpose. A base layer might consist of a simple drum loop to establish rhythm, while additional layers could include melodic elements, ambient sounds, or vocal snippets. These layers interact dynamically, complementing and contrasting with each other to produce a nuanced sonic landscape. By carefully adjusting the levels and effects of each layer, producers can highlight particular elements, guiding the listener's attention through the track.

Layering also helps create a sense of space within the music. By placing different elements at varying volumes and positions in the stereo field, producers can craft an auditory environment that feels expansive and three-dimensional.

Incorporation of Ambient Sounds

Ambient sounds play a crucial role in shaping the atmospheric quality of lo-fi music. They add a layer of depth and character that can transform an ordinary track into something truly immersive. *Field recordings*, for instance, are commonly used by lo-fi producers to create unique sonic environments. These recordings capture everyday sounds—be it the hum of city traffic, the chirping of birds, or the rustle of leaves—that, when woven into a track, make the listener feel enveloped in a specific environment.

Field recordings form the backbone of these immersive experiences. Imagine a lo-fi track that begins with the gentle patter of rain tapping against a window. This simple addition immediately sets a mood and transports the listener to a cozy, rainy afternoon. The subtle interplay of these sounds with the main melody creates a profoundly engaging atmosphere (Murahari et al., 2022). By incorporating field recordings, lo-fi artists can evoke a sense of place and time, making their music not just something to listen to but something to experience.

The use of ambient noises aren't limited to natural settings; urban sounds also find their way into lo-fi tracks. The distant chatter of a café, the soft clanging of dishes, or even the muffled announcements from a train station can all contribute to an authentic and nostalgic vibe. These ambient elements act as emotional triggers, bringing memories and feelings to the forefront as listeners get lost in the music.

Using *natural sounds* is another powerful technique in lo-fi production. The beauty of this genre lies in its ability to turn mundane, everyday sounds into something magical. For example, the sound of waves crashing on a shore can be layered under a mellow piano melody, instantly evoking a sense of calm and tranquility. Nature sounds have an inherent soothing quality, making them perfect for the relaxed, laid-back mood that lo-fi music aims to achieve.

Urban environments also provide a rich tapestry of sounds that can enhance the mood of lo-fi tracks. The gentle hum of evening traffic, distant sirens, or the rhythmic clacking of keyboards can add a unique texture to the music. These sounds ground the music in reality, giving it a lived-in feel that resonates with listeners. It's like adding a touch of real life into the dreamy soundscapes, making the experience more relatable and intimate.

Everyday life sounds, such as footsteps, doors creaking, or wind chimes, can be subtly integrated into lo-fi tracks. These sounds are familiar yet often overlooked, and their inclusion can create a comforting sense of familiarity. By blending these ambient sounds seamlessly into the music, lo-fi artists can craft a more immersive and emotional listening experience.

Blending ambient textures within lo-fi compositions is an art form in itself. The key is to integrate these sounds in a way that they complement rather than overpower the main musical elements. Subtlety is essential; the ambient sounds should enhance the overall mood without drawing too much attention to themselves.

For instance, a lo-fi track might feature a soft, repetitive guitar loop accompanied by the faint sound of a crackling fireplace. The ambient texture of the fire adds warmth and coziness to the composition, making it perfect for unwinding. The skillful blending of these textures can turn an ordinary track into an evocative piece of auditory art, where each element complements the other to create a harmonious whole.

Ambient textures can also be layered to build complexity within a track. Multiple layers of sound—like distant thunder, rustling leaves, and soft whispers—can create a rich tapestry that engages the listener's senses on multiple levels. Each listen might reveal new details, making the music an ever-evolving experience. This approach adds depth and makes the tracks more dynamic and interesting.

Creating auditory landscapes is perhaps the most captivating aspect of using ambient sounds in lo-fi music. These landscapes paint vivid pictures in the listener's mind, transporting them to different worlds. An auditory landscape could be as simple as a serene park scene with birds singing and leaves rustling or as complex as a bustling cityscape with overlapping conversations and traffic noise.

The role of ambient sounds in crafting these landscapes cannot be overstated. They serve as the foundation upon which the entire sonic environment is built. When done well, these auditory landscapes can evoke strong emotional responses, from nostalgia and comfort to introspection and peace. The power of these landscapes lies in their ability to make the listener feel present in a different place, even if only for the duration of the track.

These auditory landscapes can also serve as a form of escapism for the listener. In a fast-paced world filled with constant distractions and stressors, lo-fi music offers a brief respite. The carefully crafted soundscapes allow listeners to lose themselves in a different reality, providing a mental break and promoting relaxation (Murahari et al., 2022).

Importance of Simplistic Instrumentation

Minimalistic instrumentation contributes significantly to lo-fi music's distinctive sound and relaxed ambiance. By embracing simplicity, musicians can create a calming and inviting atmosphere that defines the genre. The beauty of minimalistic instrumental arrangements lies in their ability to evoke emotions without overwhelming the listener with complex or excessive sounds.

In lo-fi music, less is often more. Simplifying the instrumental setup helps to highlight the subtle nuances and imperfections that give the genre its unique charm. Musicians focus on a few key instruments, carefully selecting and arranging them to produce a cohesive and soothing soundscape. This artistic choice not only enables the listener to appreciate the individual characteristics of each instrument but also fosters an intimate and personal listening experience.

The lo-fi aesthetic thrives on the stripped-down nature of its compositions. By reducing the number of elements in a track, producers can draw attention to the textures and timbres that define the genre. This minimalistic approach encourages listeners to engage more deeply with the music, appreciating the understated beauty of its simplicity. Embracing simplicity is a deliberate choice that enhances the laid-back vibe lo-fi music aims to achieve, making it a perfect companion for relaxation, study, or introspection.

A fundamental aspect of lo-fi music production is the focus on basic instrumentals. Simple instruments like keyboards, guitars, and drum machines form the backbone of many lo-fi tracks. They provide a solid foundation upon which the rest of the composition is built. These instruments are chosen for their versatility and ability to convey a wide range of emotions with minimal technical complexity.

Keyboards are often used in lo-fi music because they produce warm, nostalgic tones that complement the genre's laid-back vibe. Whether it's a vintage electric piano or a modern synthesizer, the keyboard's sound can be tailored to fit the specific mood of the track. Guitars, both acoustic and electric, add a layer of organic texture to lo-fi compositions. Their mellow strumming patterns and gentle melodies contribute to the overall sense of calm and relaxation that defines the genre.

Drum machines play a crucial role in shaping the rhythmic structure of lo-fi music. By using simple beats and loops, producers can create a steady, unobtrusive rhythm that supports the other elements of the track without overpowering them. This approach allows the listener to focus on the melodic and harmonic aspects of the music, further enhancing the soothing effect of the minimalistic instrumentation.

Layering with restraint is another key principle in lo-fi music production. While adding layers can create depth and richness, it's important to maintain the simplicity that characterizes the genre. Producers need to strike a balance between enriching the track with additional elements and preserving the minimalistic aesthetic that defines lo-fi music. This delicate equilibrium ensures that the music remains accessible and enjoyable without becoming cluttered or overwhelming.

One of the most effective techniques for layering with restraint is to use *subtle variations and textures* rather than introducing entirely new instruments or sounds. For example, a producer might add a faint echo to a guitar melody or incorporate a soft background hum to create a sense of depth without disrupting the central theme of the track. These small touches enhance the overall atmosphere of the music while keeping the arrangement minimal and cohesive.

Another important consideration when layering in lo-fi music is the *placement and timing* of each element. By carefully arranging the different layers and ensuring they complement one another, producers can create a harmonious blend that maintains the genre's signature simplicity. This approach not only preserves the integrity of the music but also allows listeners to appreciate the individual contributions of each layer.

Simplistic instrumentation in lo-fi music creates space for lo-fi audio qualities to shine through. By limiting the number of elements in a track, producers can accentuate the imperfections and analog warmth that give the genre its distinctive character. This space allows the subtle nuances of tape hiss, vinyl crackle, and other lo-fi artifacts to become an integral part of the listening experience, adding depth and texture to the music.

The presence of these lo-fi elements adds a layer of authenticity and nostalgia to lo-fi music, evoking memories of older recording technologies and simpler times. The imperfections and quirks in the sound quality create a sense of intimacy, as if the listener is hearing a personal, handcrafted creation rather than a polished, commercial product. This connection between the listener and the music is a hallmark of the Lo-fi genre, and it is made possible by the intentional use of simplistic instrumentation.

Effects of Lo-fi Audio Quality

Lo-fi music embraces imperfections, and that's what makes it so special. The warm, vintage sound comes from tape hiss, vinyl crackles, and gentle distortions. These "flaws" might seem like problems, but they actually add character and personality to the music.

When you hear those familiar pops and crackles, you're taken back in time. The nostalgia creates an emotional connection that perfect digital recordings can't match. The casual, unpolished vibe also makes lo-fi music really inviting and relaxing to listen to.

Noise and distortion aren't just accidents in Lo-fi—they're artistic choices. These artists use these sounds deliberately to build a rich, textured atmosphere. It's all about finding the right balance, where the imperfections complement the music instead of overpowering it.

Embracing flaws is at the heart of Lo-fi. Unlike mainstream music, lo-fi artists don't try to make everything perfect. The occasional off-note or background chatter adds to the charm and authenticity. These imperfections tell a story and make the music feel more human and relatable.

This DIY, imperfect approach also makes lo-fi music accessible. Anybody with basic tools and creativity can get involved. It's not about technical perfection but about capturing the right mood and feeling.

So, the next time you hear that warm crackle or subtle hiss in a lo-fi track, remember—it's not a flaw, it's a feature. Those imperfections are what give the music its unique character and make it so special.

Key Takeaways

- Exploration of the various production techniques that make lo-fi music unique, including sampling/looping, ambient sounds, simplistic instrumentation, and lo-fi audio quality.
- These elements work together to create a nostalgic and comforting listening experience.
- Lo-fi producers skillfully blend the old with the new, using vintage samples, ambient sounds, and minimalist instruments

to craft timeless soundscapes.

- The intricate balance between simplicity and complexity in lo-fi music is about creating a personal, intimate experience for the listener.
- Though the "imperfections" are celebrated, some wonder if Lo-fi's rough edges could deter mainstream acceptance in a culture that often strives for polished perfection.
- However, Lo-fi's raw and authentic feel might challenge these norms and encourage a more relaxed, genuine listening experience.
- Lo-fi's rise reflects a shift in listener preferences, as people seek out music that provides comfort and serves as a backdrop for daily life.
- Lo-fi effortlessly bridges the past and present, offering something fresh yet familiar.
- The open-ended questions about Lo-fi's future concern whether it will maintain its underground appeal or break into the mainstream further, and how upcoming producers will innovate within the genre?

Chapter 5

How Lo-fi Music Is Consumed by Its Audience

When it comes to the enduring appeal of lo-fi music, there's a lot more to unpack than just the genre's signature sound. The raw, imperfect quality is a big part of what draws people in. When you start exploring the ways Lo-fi is discovered, experienced, and integrated into people's lives, a more nuanced picture emerges.

Platforms like Spotify, YouTube, and SoundCloud have made lo-fi music more accessible, thanks to their curated playlists and algorithm-powered recommendations. These tools don't just help listeners find new lo-fi artists and tracks—they shape their preferences and listening behaviors.

If you're someone who's just getting into Lo-fi, the playlist you stumble upon on Spotify could very well determine the specific sounds and vibes you end up gravitating toward. As you keep exploring, the platform's recommendations will continue nudging you in certain directions, introducing you to related artists and deepening your connection to the genre.

With a platform like SoundCloud, the sense of community and

collaboration between lo-fi artists and fans is a big part of the draw. It's a more intimate, grassroots kind of experience where you can dive deep into the stories and creative processes behind the music.

Ultimately, what makes lo-fi music so captivating is how it fits into people's lives in deeply personal, multifaceted ways. The more you explore, the more you start to appreciate the diversity of the genre.

The journey of discovering Lo-fi isn't only about appreciating the music itself; it's also about understanding how it integrates with our modern, digital-driven lives in unique ways.

Streaming Trends and Platform Preferences

Understanding where and how lo-fi music is mostly consumed can shed light on its popularity and reach. Audiences worldwide access lo-fi music on platforms like Spotify, YouTube, and SoundCloud.

Spotify

Spotify has become a go-to destination for Lo-fi music fans, and it's easy to see why. The platform offers a treasure trove of lo-fi-centric playlists that cater to all sorts of moods and activities.

Take the "Lo-fi Beats" playlist, for example—it's got over 5 million followers and is gaining more every day. That's a testament to just how popular and widespread the demand for soothing, atmospheric lo-fi tunes has become.

The platform's algorithm-powered recommendations are also incredibly effective at introducing listeners to new artists and songs within the genre. Based on your listening history, Spotify can surface all sorts of hidden gems that you might have otherwise missed.

It's like having your own personal Lo-fi concierge, always on the lookout for the next great track to add to your queue. You start off listening to a few familiar favorites, and before you know it, your Discover Weekly playlist is filled with all kinds of fresh lo-fi sounds that you can't wait to dive into.

Spotify's Lo-fi ecosystem also caters to any kind of listener. Whether you're a hardcore collector searching for those rare, obscure gems or you're just looking for a reliable source of mellow, study-friendly beats, the platform's got you covered.

Ultimately, Spotify has become such a hub for lo-fi fans because it makes the music so accessible and discoverable.

YouTube

YouTube offers an immersive, interactive environment where lo-fi music really comes alive.

Take a channel like ChilledCow, for example—they've got this 24/7 Lo-fi live stream that's the musical equivalent of a cozy, animated movie theater. You get soothing, atmospheric beats playing non-stop, paired with fantastic, lo-fi-inspired visuals that just pull you right into the music.

The best part is the sense of community that these Lo-fi YouTube channels foster. You're not just listening to the music in isolation—you're part of a lively, engaged group of lo-fi fans, who chat and connect in real-time. It's a virtual lo-fi hangout spot, where everyone comes together to share their love of the genre.

The community aspect is important, because it really heightens the whole listening experience. When you've got fellow lo-fi enthusiasts hyping up their favorite tracks, or swapping recommendations in the comments, it makes you feel like you're part of something bigger. It's not just about the music—it's about the culture and the shared appreciation for those warm, imperfect sounds.

The interactivity of these YouTube channels also means you can get a more personal connection to the artists themselves. A lot of these lo-fi producers will pop into the chat, respond to comments, and even give little behind-the-scenes insights into their creative process. It's a level of access and engagement that you just don't get with a lot of other music platforms.

YouTube's Lo-fi scene is about immersing yourself in this vibrant, interconnected world of lo-fi enthusiasts who come together to celebrate the genre's unique charms.

SoundCloud

SoundCloud is focused on empowering artists and fostering a more organic, community-driven music discovery experience.

SoundCloud makes it easy for lo-fi producers—both established and up-and-coming—to share their creations directly with listeners. You don't need a huge budget or fancy recording equipment to get your music out there. All you need is a SoundCloud account and the drive to create. It's a level playing field that really celebrates the DIY spirit at the heart of the lo-fi scene.

The direct artist-to-fan connection is a big part of what makes the SoundCloud experience so unique. Instead of relying on algorithm-driven recommendations or curated playlists, listeners on the platform tend to discover new lo-fi artists through good old-fashioned word of mouth. They'll see their favorite producers reposting songs, or they'll stumble upon expertly curated sets from trusted lo-fi influencers. It's a much more grassroots, community-driven way of finding new music.

The SoundCloud approach is about exploring, digging deeper, and really connecting with the artists behind the music. You get a more intimate, authentic experience rather than just having stuff fed to you based on your listening history.

The emphasis on artist support is crucial, especially for up-and-coming lo-fi producers trying to build a fanbase. On SoundCloud, your fans can directly engage with your music, leave comments, and even repost your tracks to share with their own networks. It's a super interactive, collaborative ecosystem that helps fuel the genre's grassroots growth.

The SoundCloud platform really puts the music and the community first rather than just optimizing for streams and algorithm-driven hits.

User Engagement Patterns

Each platform has its own unique ways of attracting and retaining listeners. Spotify's seamless playlist integration and personalized recommendations offer a structured yet tailored listening experience. Users appreciate how easy it is to discover new music through automated suggestions.

YouTube's approach involves mixing music with visuals, creating a multisensory experience that engages viewers beyond just audio. The ability to watch calming animations or scenery while listening to lo-fi beats makes YouTube a preferred choice for many. Moreover, the communal aspect, where listeners can interact in real-time or leave comments, also makes the listening experience more social.

SoundCloud stands out due to its role in promoting upcoming artists. The platform's functionality encourages sharing and collaboration among creators and fans. For many listeners, part of the appeal lies in supporting independent artists and discovering unique tracks that might not be available on larger streaming services.

Highlighting the differences in user engagement across various platforms helps illustrate why some listeners may prefer one service over another. Spotify's data-driven model provides an efficient and personalized music discovery process, appealing to those who enjoy curated experiences. On YouTube, the visual components and community interactions are major draws for individuals who want more than just music.

SoundCloud's emphasis on artist empowerment and discovery resonates with listeners interested in staying close to the creative pulse of the Lo-fi scene. Its community-driven atmosphere supports a more intimate connection between artists and fans. Each platform's unique strengths cater to different aspects of the listener's desires, whether they seek efficiency, community, or discovery.

Playlist Curation

When it comes to discovering and enjoying lo-fi music, curated playlists are pretty much essential. They're like these carefully crafted gateways that make it so much easier to explore the genre and find the sounds you love.

With so much amazing lo-fi music out there, it can be a little overwhelming trying to figure out where to start. This is where curated playlists step in and do the heavy lifting for you. Whether it's on Spotify, YouTube, or other smaller platforms, the folks behind these playlists have put in the work to sift through all the tracks and compile the best of the best.

The great thing is that these playlists don't just feature the big, well-known lo-fi hits. They also showcase tons of hidden gems and up-and-coming artists that you might not have stumbled upon otherwise. It's the perfect blend of the familiar and the fresh, and it keeps your listening experience engaging.

On YouTube, for example, you've got channels like College Music and Chillhop Music that curate these killer lo-fi playlists. They really dive deep into the different subgenres and styles within the Lo-fi realm, so you can find the vibe that speaks to you—whether that's jazzy, instrumental-focused tracks, or something a little more lo-fi and beat-driven.

And on Spotify, the platform's algorithm-powered recommendations play a huge role in surfacing new lo-fi music that aligns with your personal tastes. It's like having your own personal music concierge, constantly introducing you to tracks and artists you're going to love. The more you listen, the smarter the recommendations get.

Ultimately, what makes these curated playlists so valuable is the way they simplify the discovery process. Instead of having to sift through thousands of tracks and wonder what's worth checking out, you've got these expertly crafted lists that do all the hard work for you. It's a guided experience that's especially helpful for new Lo-fi fans who are just discovering the genre.

Once you find a playlist you really enjoy, you can just let it ride and enjoy that consistent, cohesive Lo-fi experience. You no longer have to jump from track to track, constantly trying to figure out what to listen to next.

Popular Lo-fi Playlists and Channels

Prominent lo-fi playlists like "Chill Beats" and "Lo-fi Study Mix" are mainstays on major streaming platforms such as Spotify, YouTube, and Apple Music.

The characteristics and themes of these popular playlists typically emphasize calm, instrumental beats with influences from jazz, hip-hop, and ambient music. "Chill Beats" often includes tracks with smooth, repetitive rhythms and mellow tones designed to create a relaxed, focused atmosphere. Similarly, "Lo-fi Study Mix" features songs aimed at helping listeners concentrate, using soothing sounds and gentle melodies. These playlists often incorporate ambient noises, such as raindrops or soft vinyl crackles, to enhance the nostalgic and comforting feel of the music (Criscuolo, 2022).

Playlist placement offers real financial implications for the artists as well. When your track starts racking up those playlist streams, that translates directly to royalty income. And the visibility can open all sorts of other doors, from growing your social media following to landing sponsorship deals and live performance gigs.

The platforms themselves even offer artists a range of promotional tools and analytics to help them make the most of this playlist exposure. They can see exactly who's listening to their music, where they're from, and how engaged they are. That kind of data-driven insight is gold when it comes to developing effective marketing strategies and reaching new fans.

And speaking of sponsors, that's another way these lo-fi playlists can really pay off for artists. When your track starts blowing up on a popular playlist, it can catch the eye of brands and companies looking to tap into that laid-back, creative vibe. Next thing you know, you're getting offers to create sponsored content or collaborate on special projects.

Ultimately, what makes these curated lo-fi playlists so powerful is the way they combine music discovery, artist support, and monetization opportunities. They're not just passive listening experiences—they're dynamic ecosystems that are constantly evolving and creating new opportunities for lo-fi creators to shine.

Demographics of Lo-fi Listeners

When it comes to the world of lo-fi music, it's fascinating to see how the genre has captured the attention of listeners across different age groups, genders, and cultural backgrounds. It's truly a global phenomenon that seems to resonate with people in all kinds of unique ways.

One of the groups that Lo-fi has really resonated with is the younger crowd of teens and up through the early 20s. It's easy to see why this demographic has taken such a strong liking to the genre. Lo-fi's calming, mellow beats provide the perfect backdrop for all the studying, unwinding, and general life-navigating that this age group is doing. There's just something about those nostalgic, lo-fi textures that feel so soothing and comforting amidst the chaos of everyday life.

The genre seems to have a universal appeal that cuts across traditional gender lines as well. Both men and women seem to appreciate the ambient, atmospheric qualities of Lo-fi—though you might notice some slight variations in their preferences. The ladies might gravitate more towards the melodic, softer aspects of the music, while the men enjoy the rhythmic, percussive elements.

Lo-fi has a diverse global reach. In places like the US, Japan, and Germany—cities with big student populations and buzzing online communities—it has become especially popular.

Beyond the student hubs, Lo-fi has made serious inroads in places like the UK and South Korea, largely thanks to the rise of streaming platforms like YouTube and Spotify. The way these services have made Lo-fi music so accessible has been a total game-changer, introducing the genre to new audiences around the world.

As Lo-fi has spread to different cultures, you start to see these really fascinating regional variations emerge. Moreover, in Japan, for instance, you'll find Lo-fi tracks that incorporate traditional instrumentation and local soundscapes, giving the music this really unique, place-specific flavor. In the West, the lo-fi aesthetic tends to pull more from jazz and hip-hop influences, reflecting those local musical tastes.

In the end, what makes lo-fi music so captivating is its ability to transcend all sorts of demographic and cultural boundaries. Whether you're a stressed-out student in Berlin or a seasoned music fan in Seoul, there's something about those warm, imperfect sounds that speak to the human experience on a universal level. Finally, it's a genre that connects people across the globe, fostering a sense of community and shared appreciation.

Unique Listening Behaviors

Lo-fi music has become ingrained in so many people's daily routines, and it's easy to see why. The genre's soothing, unobtrusive soundscapes make it the perfect companion for a whole range of activities, from studying and working to unwinding at home.

One of the biggest reasons Lo-fi is so popular is its ability to enhance focus and concentration without being overly distracting. Compared to more upbeat or lyrically driven music, those soft beats and mellow melodies just seem to fade into the background, allowing you to stay locked in on the task at hand. That's why you'll find so many students turning to Lo-fi playlists during long study sessions—it keeps them grounded and productive without pulling their attention away.

Lo-fi's applications go way beyond just academic or professional settings. It's also a go-to choice for all sorts of leisure activities, like reading, cooking, or even hosting social gatherings. The music has this inherent calming quality that helps create the perfect relaxed atmosphere without ever feeling like it's taking center stage.

Many people turn to Lo-fi specifically for its stress-relieving properties. After a long, hectic day, there's nothing quite like kicking back and letting those soothing, ambient sounds wash over you. It's like having your own little oasis of tranquility where you can truly decompress and unwind.

The way Lo-fi integrates into different environments is pretty fascinating. You'll often hear it playing in cozy cafes or bookstores, subtly enhancing the music without ever becoming too obtrusive or overpowering. It's the sonic equivalent of that perfect cup of coffee or comfy reading nook—it just feels right.

One of the most interesting Lo-fi consumption habits is the trend of repeat playbacks and extended listening sessions. Many fans just love to let their favorite tracks or playlists loop endlessly, finding a real sense of comfort and flow in the repetitive nature of the music. It's like aural meditation, allowing your mind to fully immerse itself and stay focused, whether you're working, studying, or just relaxing.

Ultimately, what makes Lo-fi such a staple in so many people's lives is the way it manages to enhance productivity, relaxation, and everything in between. It's music that just seems to seamlessly integrate into your daily routine, providing the perfect auditory accompaniment no matter what you're up to. And when you consider the calming, almost therapeutic effects of that repetitive, ambient sound, it's no wonder Lo-fi has become such an essential part of so many listeners' lives.

Key Takeaways

- Spotify uses algorithms to recommend new lo-fi tracks tailored to individual preferences.
- YouTube combines the music with visuals, creating a relaxing, communal environment.
- SoundCloud empowers both established and emerging artists to share their work.
- Curated playlists play a pivotal role in shaping the Lo-fi listening experience.
- Carefully curated selections like "Chill Beats" on Spotify serve as go-to spaces for relaxation and focus.
- Algorithms personalize the recommendations, helping listeners discover new music.
- Lo-fi has a broad appeal that transcends demographics.
- Resonates with a diverse audience, from teenagers to young adults, and across cultures and genders.
- Has a global fanbase, with particularly strong pockets in countries like the US, Japan, and Germany.
- The genre even adapts locally, incorporating traditional sounds.
- Lo-fi integrates seamlessly into people's daily lives.
- Provides unobtrusive background music for activities like studying, working, and cooking.
- The power of repetition helps listeners concentrate and relax by looping favorite tracks.
- Communal and interactive features on platforms like YouTube add another layer to the experience.
- Live chats and comment sections foster a sense of belonging among fans.

- SoundCloud's artist-centric approach encourages listeners to discover and support independent musicians.
- Understanding Lo-fi consumption trends provides insights into broader shifts in the music industry.
- This highlights a growing demand for more personalized and immersive listening experiences.
- It could have far-reaching implications for how people engage with different musical genres.

Chapter 6

The Role of Lo-fi Music Within the Wider Music Industry

The fascinating thing about lo-fi music is how it's managed to transcend the boundaries of its own genre and start popping up all over the broader music landscape. It's like this mellow, atmospheric sound that's just infusing itself into all kinds of different styles, breathing new life into them and creating some seriously exciting new hybrids.

Take pop music, for example. Artists take those soothing, laid-back lo-fi beats and layer them over catchy melodies and hooks, giving the whole thing this really warm, nostalgic vibe. It's like they're taking the polished sheen of pop and then kind of roughing it up a little bit, turning it into something that feels a lot more authentic and emotionally resonant.

In the world of hip-hop, Lo-fi's influence is just as profound. Producers sample those crackling vinyl textures, weave them into the beats, and then rappers do their thing on top. The result is this captivating fusion of old-school grit and modern sensibilities—it's like you're getting the best of both worlds, all wrapped up in one killer track.

It's not just the urban genres that feel the impact of Lo-fi. Even in the realms of electronic and rock music, you can hear those mellow, atmospheric qualities seeping in and adding a whole new dimension. Suddenly, those pulsing synthesizers or crunchy guitar riffs have this extra layer of warmth and depth to them, making the music feel more inviting and organic.

A big part of what's driving this whole Lo-fi crossover phenomenon is the genre's universal appeal. Those calming, nostalgic vibes just seem to resonate with listeners on such a primal level, regardless of their usual musical tastes. It's like Lo-fi has this magical ability to enhance whatever style of music it touches, elevating the emotional impact and creating something that's both familiar and fresh.

So, whether you're a pop diehard, a hip-hop head, or a hardcore rocker, chances are you've been feeling the Lo-fi influence creeping into your favorite music.

Interaction with Other Music Genres

Lo-fi musicians often collaborate with mainstream artists. They have teamed up with pop, rock, and other genre artists to produce hybrid tracks that blend the mellow beats of Lo-fi with more mainstream sounds. For instance, the collaboration between lo-fi artist Idealism and pop singer H.E.R. created a unique track that fused soothing lo-fi beats with soulful pop vocals. Such collaborations showcase how Lo-fi can complement and enhance various musical styles.

The collaboration between rock band Tame Impala and lo-fi producer Tomppa Beats is also a notable example. By merging psychedelic-rock elements with chilled-out lo-fi beats, they crafted a track that resonated with fans from both genres. These hybrid creations not only highlight the adaptability of lo-fi music but also open new avenues for artists to experiment and reach broader audiences.

These collaborations are not just one-off experiments; they represent a broader trend of genre-blending in the music industry. As Lo-fi continues to gain popularity, more artists from diverse backgrounds are likely to explore its potential. The result is a rich tapestry of sounds that appeal to a wide range of listeners, demonstrating Lo-fi's capacity to bring together seemingly disparate musical worlds in a harmonious blend.

Lo-fi music's influence on pop and hip-hop productions has become increasingly apparent in recent years. Mainstream pop songs often incorporate lo-fi beats to add a laid-back, atmospheric quality. For example, artists like Billie Eilish use subtle lo-fi elements to create a haunting, introspective vibe in her music that sets it apart from the rest of the pop scene.

Similarly, hip-hop producers have embraced lo-fi beats to infuse their tracks with a nostalgic, relaxed feel. The use of ambient sounds and simple, repetitive drum patterns common in lo-fi music can be heard in the works of artists such as J. Cole and Kendrick Lamar. By integrating these elements, hip-hop tracks gain a unique flavor that enhances the lyrical depth and emotional resonance of the songs. This blending of genres showcases how lo-fi music is shaping contemporary production styles, making it a staple in modern studios.

The trend of incorporating lo-fi elements into pop and hip-hop demonstrates the genre's widespread appeal and its ability to adapt to different musical contexts. It also highlights the evolving nature of music production, where producers continuously seek out new sounds and textures to keep their work fresh and engaging. Lo-fi music, with its distinctive aesthetic and vibe, provides an invaluable resource for this creative process.

Lo-fi music has also found a home within electronic music genres, moving beyond pop and hip-hop. The fusion of lo-fi elements with electronic music, such as house and techno, creates exciting new subgenres that captivate listeners. Producers like Kaytranada seamlessly blend lo-fi beats with electronic rhythms, resulting in tracks that are both danceable and mellow, offering a unique listening experience. This combination leads to the creation of music that can soothe and energize simultaneously, appealing to a broad audience.

Electronic music often thrives on innovation, and the inclusion of lo-fi elements adds another layer of experimentation. Chopped samples and chill beats characteristic of lo-fi music bring a sense of warmth and nostalgia to otherwise high-energy tracks. This fusion can be heard in the works of artists like Bonobo, who expertly mix lo-fi textures with electronic soundscapes to craft immersive auditory experiences. The blending process leads to the emergence of fresh sounds that push the boundaries of traditional electronic music.

The cross-pollination of Lo-fi and electronic music not only expands the sonic possibilities for producers but also enriches the listener's experience. It encourages fans of one genre to explore another, which will deepen their appreciation of the diverse range of music that's available. This fusion exemplifies how lo-fi music serves as a bridge connecting various musical realms, promoting creativity and innovation across the industry.

One remarkable aspect of lo-fi music is its cross-genre appeal. Its mellow tones and relaxing vibes attract a diverse audience, cutting across traditional genre lines. Listeners who typically favor intense genres like metal or energetic ones like pop find solace in the calming effects of lo-fi music. This broad appeal is evident in the growing number of lo-fi playlists on streaming platforms, which are frequented by users from various musical backgrounds seeking a tranquil listening experience.

Presence at Music Festivals and Events

When you think of music festivals, the first thing that usually comes to mind is high-energy, adrenaline-pumping performances—the kind that gets the crowds jumping and dancing. In recent years, we've seen the rise of a new festival experience, one that's a little more chilled-out and introspective: the lo-fi music stage.

Now, these lo-fi sets might not have the same heart-pounding, fist-pumping vibe as some of the main stage acts, but they offer something truly special. Instead of trying to hype up the crowd, the artists are focused on creating this soothing, immersive atmosphere—the kind that makes you want to just kick back, relax, and let the music wash over you.

At a lo-fi stage, you'll see people sprawled out on blankets, eyes closed, just nodding their heads gently to the beat. It's a much more subdued, personal kind of engagement compared to the collective euphoria you'd find at a typical festival set. This is the magic of Lo-fi—it has this incredible power to forge a deep, individual connection with the listener.

The fact that these lo-fi stages are popping up at major festivals like Coachella and Glastonbury shows how much the genre has grown in popularity and legitimacy. It's no longer just some niche, underground thing—it's a bona fide part of the live music landscape, catering to all those festivalgoers who are craving a more calming, meditative experience.

The Lo-fi influence extends beyond just the stage performances. You'll also find these mellow, atmospheric tracks being used to enhance the overall festival vibe, whether it's playing in the chill-out zones or providing a soothing auditory backdrop between the high-energy sets. It's all about creating this well-rounded, balanced experience that caters to a wide range of attendee preferences.

The really special thing about lo-fi festivals is the way they foster a sense of community among the fans. It's not just about passive listening—it's about connecting with like-minded people who share your appreciation for those warm, nostalgic sounds. The laid-back, approachable nature of the performances helps break down barriers between the artists and the audience, creating this really intimate, inclusive vibe.

The communal aspect of lo-fi music has even made the jump to the digital realm, with virtual lo-fi streams and events bringing people together from all around the world. This is a testament to the genre's power to unite music lovers regardless of geographic boundaries.

In many ways, the rise of lo-fi music in the festival space represents a shift in the broader live music culture. It's about acknowledging the need for balance, for moments of calm and introspection amidst all the excitement and euphoria. As festivals continue to evolve and diversify their offerings, you can bet that Lo-fi is going to play an increasingly important role in shaping that holistic, well-rounded attendee experience.

Lo-fi Music in Film and Television

Lo-fi music has found a niche within the audiovisual medium, particularly in the realm of soundtracks and scores for films and television.

Directors and composers often use lo-fi tracks to set a particular mood or theme within various scenes. This genre's ability to evoke feelings of nostalgia, tranquility, or introspection makes it an ideal choice for storytelling. For instance, a scene depicting a character's contemplation, or a reflective montage might be accompanied by lo-fi background music, subtly influencing the viewer's emotional response.

In recent years, several filmmakers have recognized the potential of lo-fi music to enrich their narratives. Shows like *Euphoria* and movies such as *Lady Bird* have integrated lo-fi elements into their soundtracks, creating a more immersive experience for audiences. By layering lo-fi rhythms over critical moments, these productions not only enhance the storyline but also provide viewers with a musical experience that complements the visual content. It's a testament to how versatile and adaptive lo-fi music can be in different storytelling contexts.

The integration of lo-fi music into soundtracks has opened new avenues for composers. Traditional scoring techniques often rely on grand orchestral pieces, but Lo-fi offers a minimalistic yet impactful alternative. Composers are now blending Lo-fi's simplistic beats with conventional scoring methods, resulting in a hybrid soundscape that is both innovative and emotionally engaging. This trend is likely to continue growing as more creators explore the versatility of Lo-fi in enhancing cinematic storytelling.

The aesthetic appeal of lo-fi music lies in its nostalgic and soothing qualities. Many listeners say lo-fi tracks remind them of simpler times, often evoking memories of late-night study sessions or lazy afternoons. These characteristics make Lo-fi an attractive option for visual media, where the goal is often to create a specific atmosphere or emotional tone. Lo-fi music can make a scene more relatable and heartfelt.

When used in visual media, lo-fi music helps establish an emotional connection between the audience and the characters. For example, a scene showing a character's journey home after a long day paired with a lo-fi track can make the moment feel more intimate and authentic. The genre's unpolished and raw vibe adds depth to the narrative, allowing viewers to immerse themselves fully in the story being told. It's no wonder that Lo-fi has become a staple in many indie films and web series aiming for an authentic, grounded feel.

Beyond individual scenes, the overall tone of a film or series can benefit from the consistent inclusion of lo-fi music. Its calming influence can act as a thread that ties various parts of the narrative together. By selecting tracks that reflect the overarching themes of the story, creators can subtly guide viewers through the emotional landscape of the plot, ensuring a more profound and lasting impact.

There has been a noticeable trend in recent years where filmmakers incorporate lo-fi elements into their compositions. This emerging trend reflects a shift in storytelling techniques, where traditional barriers between genres are being blurred. Films and TV shows keen on staying relevant and edgy are increasingly adopting lo-fi music to keep pace with contemporary tastes. Shows like *BoJack Horseman* and *Stranger Things* have used lo-fi-inspired soundscapes.

Independent filmmakers and smaller production houses can easily incorporate lo-fi elements without the need for extensive orchestral arrangements or high-budget studios. This accessibility means there can be more experimentation and innovation with the way stories are told through the music. Lo-fi's uncomplicated structure gives filmmakers the freedom to play with mood and tone in ways that were previously too expensive.

As Lo-fi continues to grow in popularity, we can expect even more inventive uses of the genre in film scoring. Whether it's in mainstream cinema or independent projects, the adaptability of Lo-fi ensures it will remain a valuable tool for creators looking to connect with their audiences on a deeper level. This evolving trend highlights the genre's potential to redefine traditional storytelling methods and pave the way for new artistic expressions.

Cultural references and contemporary themes often find a voice through lo-fi music in visual media. This genre's flexibility allows it to seamlessly integrate diverse cultural nuances, making it a powerful tool in both Western and non-Western content. For instance, anime series like *Cowboy Bebop* and *Samurai Champloo* have successfully incorporated lo-fi elements, resonating with global audiences and reflecting Japan's rich cultural heritage.

By embedding lo-fi tracks within a storyline, creators can subtly comment on societal issues or depict everyday life in a way that feels current and relevant. Western media has also embraced this approach, with shows set in urban environments using Lo-fi to mirror the hustle and bustle of city life or the quiet moments that punctuate it. The genre's ability to straddle different cultures and contexts makes it uniquely suited for storytelling across various platforms.

Lo-fi's cross-cultural appeal has also led to collaborations that bring distinct musical traditions into the fold. Producers combine traditional instruments from different cultures with modern lo-fi beats, creating a fusion that speaks to a global audience. This blend not only enriches the narrative but also introduces viewers to new sounds and perspectives, fostering a greater appreciation for cultural diversity.

Industry Recognition and Awards

As lo-fi music continues to gain mainstream recognition and acclaim, it's exciting to see the genre receiving more and more formal industry accolades. The inclusion of lo-fi-specific categories at major music awards shows just how far the genre has come in terms of legitimacy and respect.

These prestigious platforms, traditionally dominated by big, established genres like pop, rock, and hip-hop, are now making space for lo-fi artists to shine. That's a pretty big deal, and it sends a clear message that the industry is taking this genre seriously as a genuine art form worthy of critical recognition.

For the lo-fi musicians and producers who manage to nab those nominations or even take home the trophies, the benefits can be life changing. It's not just about the prestige and validation—it's about the doors that get opened. Suddenly, these artists are in the spotlight, with opportunities for bigger collaborations, sponsorships, and exposure to much wider audiences.

It's a powerful way to shatter the misconception that Lo-fi is just background music or a passing trend. When you see it earning the same level of acclaim as the mainstream heavy hitters, it really underscores the emotional depth, technical innovation, and pure artistic merit of the genre. Lo-fi is no longer the underdog—it's a legitimate, critically respected force to be reckoned with.

The positive reception from both critics and the general public has been a huge part of that shift. These respected music journalists sing the praises of lo-fi albums and songs, highlighting the genre's ability to provide comfort, focus, and genuine emotional resonance. When you pair that with the impressive chart performances and streaming numbers, it's clear that Lo-fi is striking a major chord with listeners.

Even the behind-the-scenes talents—like the lo-fi producers and sound engineers who help craft those lush, atmospheric soundscapes—are starting to get their due. When industry heavyweights shout them out or collaborate with them, it further validates just how crucial their work is to the overall lo-fi experience.

When we look ahead, there's much exciting potential for lo-fi artists to explore. Cross-genre collaborations could introduce the genre to whole new audiences, while strategic use of digital platforms and social media can help them build deeper, more engaged fanbases. Of course, the challenges of standing out in an increasingly saturated market will require a lot of creativity and resilience.

Lo-fi music is no longer the niche, underground genre it once was. It's a full-fledged art form that's earned its place at the table, commanding the same level of respect and admiration as the biggest, most established genres in the industry.

Key Takeaways

- Lo-fi music has shown great versatility by blending seamlessly with a variety of genres, including pop, rock, hip-hop, and electronic music.
- Lo-fi's incorporation into mainstream pop and hip-hop by artists like Billie Eilish and Kendrick Lamar has added depth and introspection to the productions.
- Lo-fi music has become a fixture at music festivals, offering attendees a calming presence and fostering a sense of community.
- Lo-fi's soothing beats have been used in film and television to enhance storytelling and evoke emotions.
- Lo-fi has gained industry recognition, with awards and accolades highlighting its growing legitimacy and opening doors for artists.
- Lo-fi's cross-genre appeal and adaptability make it a fascinating subject for music enthusiasts.
- The future of lo-fi music looks bright, with potential for continued innovation and integration into various musical and cultural landscapes.

Chapter 7

Future Developments and Trends in the Lo-fi Music Scene

The future of lo-fi music is bound to be fascinating, especially when you factor in all the cutting-edge technologies that are starting to shape the genre. It's like this perfect storm of creative potential, and music fans everywhere are on the edge of their seats, wondering what's going to happen next.

Take artificial intelligence (AI), for instance—researchers are already exploring ways to use artificial intelligence to generate lo-fi-inspired beats and melodies. The idea is that these AI-powered tools could help producers and artists unlock whole new realms of sonic possibilities, opening the door to all sorts of wild, experimental soundscapes. Just imagine what kind of mind-bending, genre-blending tracks could come out of that kind of collaboration between humans and machines.

There is also VR—the virtual reality tech that's been steadily gaining momentum in the music world. Lo-fi artists are starting to experiment with immersive, 360-degree experiences that can transport listeners into these cozy, nostalgic sonic environments. It's like taking that classic lo-fi vibe and cranking it up to 11, creating a fully enveloping auditory and visual experience.

It's not just the technological innovations that have lo-fi fans buzzing—it's also the potential for the genre to continue pushing the boundaries and blending with other musical styles. Producers have already been mashing up Lo-fi with everything from jazz to hip-hop, and the results are mind-blowingly good. It's like taking these familiar, comforting sounds and infusing them with new energy and fresh perspectives.

Who knows what other unexpected genre-bending experiments might be on the horizon? Maybe we'll see lo-fi artists team up with electronic dance music producers or find ways to seamlessly incorporate classical influences. The possibilities are endless, and that's what makes the future of this genre so exciting.

What is actually driving all this innovation and experimentation is the deep, unwavering passion that lo-fi fans and creators have for the music. This isn't just some fad—it's a genuine, grassroots movement fueled by people who are in love with the genre's warm, atmospheric sounds. As long as that enthusiasm keeps burning, you can bet that Lo-fi is going to continue evolving in all sorts of fascinating and unexpected ways.

Technological Advancements and Their Impact

The integration of AI in music creation is a significant recent development. It has the potential to transform how lo-fi music is composed, offering artists new tools and techniques. Using machine learning algorithms, AI can analyze existing lo-fi tracks and generate new compositions that adhere to the genre's distinct characteristics. This can help musicians produce high-quality tracks quickly and efficiently without extensive musical training. For instance, AI-generated lo-fi beats can mimic the laid-back, nostalgic atmosphere that defines the genre, providing a fresh yet authentic sound that resonates with listeners.

AI algorithms play a crucial role in mimicking the lo-fi aesthetic, making them invaluable in streamlining production processes. By analyzing various elements such as tempo, chord progressions, and ambient sounds, AI can recreate the unique soundscape of lo-fi music. This not only speeds up the production but also ensures consistency in quality. Producers can use AI tools to experiment with different textures and effects, achieving the perfect balance between polished and raw sounds that characterize lo-fi music. These algorithms can assist in mastering and mixing tracks, which can be particularly beneficial for independent artists who may lack technical expertise.

The rise of AI-generated music brings with it ethical implications regarding the authenticity of lo-fi music. One concern is whether AI-produced tracks can truly capture the human emotion and creativity that many fans value in the genre. However, there's a fear that music generated by algorithms might lack the soul and personal touch that comes from human experiences and emotions. There are also questions about the originality of AI-generated compositions, especially if they closely resemble existing works.

Another exciting frontier in the lo-fi music scene is the potential for virtual reality (VR) experiences. With VR technology, listeners can immerse themselves in a multi-sensory environment where the music comes alive in new and innovative ways. Imagine stepping into a virtual space inspired by the dreamy visuals often associated with lo-fi music videos; this could enhance the listening experience by providing a serene and visually stimulating backdrop to the calming tunes. Such immersive environments can create a stronger emotional connection between the listener and the music, transforming passive listening into an interactive, engaging experience.

VR can also open up new opportunities for lo-fi music events. Traditional concerts and performances could be reimagined within virtual spaces, allowing artists to reach a global audience without geographical constraints. This accessibility is particularly valuable for independent lo-fi artists who may not have the resources to tour extensively. VR platforms enable fans from around the world to attend virtual concerts, creating a sense of community and shared experience despite physical distances. These virtual events can feature unique visual artistry and interactive elements, enriching the overall fan experience.

Potential Shifts in Musical Style

As the lo-fi music scene continues to grow and evolve, one of the most intriguing developments is its hybridization with other genres. This fusion has already begun to take shape, blending Lo-fi's characteristic relaxed beats and nostalgic soundscapes with various contemporary styles. For example, some artists have started incorporating elements of electronic dance music (EDM), creating a unique mix that preserves Lo-fi's calming essence while introducing more dynamic, rhythmic components. This combination can bring a new layer of energy to the traditionally mellow genre, attracting listeners who enjoy both the chill vibes of Lo-fi and the upbeat tempo of EDM.

The fusion doesn't stop there. Ambient music, known for its atmospheric, immersive qualities, also offers fertile ground for hybridization with Lo-fi. By integrating ambient textures, such as ethereal synths and environmental sounds, lo-fi artists can enhance their tracks' depth and emotional resonance. This blend results in compositions that not only soothe but also transport listeners to otherworldly soundscapes, making the listening experience more engaging and immersive. As these hybrid styles gain traction, they push the boundaries of what Lo-fi can be, inviting innovation and creativity from artists across genres.

Assessing the impact of these genre crossovers on Lo-fi's overall aesthetic reveals a dynamic interplay between tradition and innovation. The core elements of Lo-fi—its simplicity, warmth, and nostalgia—remain intact, even as new influences reshape its sound. This balance ensures that the genre retains its distinctive identity while evolving to stay relevant in a rapidly changing musical landscape. Listeners benefit from this evolution, too, as it broadens their auditory horizons and introduces them to new and unexpected sonic combinations.

The exploration of experimental soundscapes is another exciting new trend in the lo-fi music scene. Artists are increasingly drawn to unconventional sounds and textures, pushing the genre into uncharted territories. This experimentation can involve anything from using field recordings of everyday noises to incorporating avant-garde production techniques. By challenging traditional Lo-fi conventions, these artists create fresh and innovative compositions that stand out in an ever-expanding musical field.

For example, some musicians have begun incorporating natural sounds like rustling leaves, running water, or distant bird calls into their tracks. These elements add a layer of authenticity and serenity, enhancing the escapist quality of lo-fi music. The use of found sounds, such as snippets of conversation or urban ambiance, can lend a track a unique character and sense of place. This approach not only diversifies the genre's sound palette but also allows artists to tell more nuanced and personal stories through their music.

By embracing the unknown and the unconventional, artists infuse their work with a spirit of adventure and curiosity. This mindset encourages continual growth and transformation within the genre, ensuring that Lo-fi remains vibrant and engaging for both creators and listeners.

Upcoming Artists and Rising Stars

The future of the lo-fi music scene is brimming with fresh talent and innovative contributions. One exciting development is the emergence of new talent hotspots around the world—cities like Los Angeles, Tokyo, and Berlin have become centers for nurturing lo-fi artists, each bringing their unique cultural flavors to the genre. Online communities also play a significant role in this growth. Platforms, such as Bandcamp and SoundCloud, allow for global collaboration and discovery, giving budding musicians a space to share their work and connect with others.

These virtual hubs foster creativity and innovation. Musicians from different backgrounds and regions come together to experiment with sounds and production techniques, further enriching the genre. For instance, lo-fi talents from Brazil are blending traditional Bossa Nova rhythms with chill beats, creating a unique subgenre that captivates listeners worldwide. This cross-pollination of ideas not only broadens the appeal of Lo-fi but also pushes its boundaries, making it an ever-evolving art form.

Senseless Optimism

Identifying and supporting upcoming artists from diverse backgrounds is integral to the lo-fi music scene's future. Artists like Senseless Optimism, who draw inspiration from their multicultural experiences, bring richness and depth to their music (VandenTop, 2020). Senseless Optimism's journey from being a percussionist in Sri Lanka to crafting introspective bedroom pop in Massachusetts exemplifies this diversity.

Her artistic journey took an unexpected turn when she moved to the United States to pursue her education at the prestigious Berklee College of Music in Boston, Massachusetts. It was there, in the confines of her bedroom, that she began experimenting with the ambient, introspective sound of lo-fi music, blending her multicultural influences into a truly captivating sonic signature.

Her music reflects the duality of her experiences—the struggles and triumphs of navigating life as a first-generation immigrant, the bitter-sweet nostalgia of her Sri Lankan roots, and the quiet contemplations that fill her day-to-day life in America. It's a deeply personal, emotionally resonant take on lo-fi that immediately connects with listeners on a profound level.

Tracks like "Rainy Day Musings" and "Autumn Leaves" showcase her talent for crafting lush, atmospheric soundscapes that envelop the listener in a warm, comforting embrace. The music taps into universal human experiences—the longing for home, the search for inner peace, the quiet moments of introspection—through a lens that is uniquely informed by her cross-cultural background.

As the lo-fi scene continues to grow and evolve, voices like Senseless Optimism's will be essential in pushing the genre to new creative heights. By sharing their diverse perspectives and lived experiences, these artists are enriching the lo-fi soundscape and making it more representative of the global community that has come to cherish the genre.

Nujabes

Artists like Nujabes have redefined Lo-fi by infusing it with elements of jazz and hip-hop, appealing to a broad audience. These musicians often come from varied geographical and cultural backgrounds, which adds layers of complexity and emotion to their creations. By sharing their unique perspectives, they contribute significantly to the genre's ongoing evolution, making it more inclusive and representative of global experiences.

The diversity within the lo-fi community also helps break down barriers and stereotypes associated with music genres. Emerging artists from underrepresented communities challenge conventional norms and bring fresh voices to the forefront.

Social media platforms have become indispensable tools for emerging lo-fi musicians looking to amplify their reach. Instagram, TikTok, and YouTube provide accessible channels for artists to showcase their work, engage with fans, and build loyal followings. The viral nature of these platforms allows unknown artists to gain overnight recognition, sometimes leading to lucrative opportunities and mainstream success.

For example, the YouTube channel Lo-fi Girl has played a pivotal role in popularizing lo-fi music. Its live streams, featuring a mix of known and unknown artists, have garnered millions of followers and views, turning it into a hub for lo-fi enthusiasts. This exposure has helped launch the careers of many independent musicians who might otherwise struggle to find an audience.

Social media encourages direct interaction between artists and their fans, creating a sense of community and loyalty. Through these platforms musicians can receive instant feedback on new releases, participate in live Q&A sessions, and even collaborate with other artists through these platforms. This level of engagement not only helps artists grow their fanbase but also allows them to maintain creative control over their work, thus preserving the authenticity that is so cherished in the Lo-fi genre.

The trend of collaborative projects among rising lo-fi artists is another significant development shaping the future of the genre. These collaborations allow musicians to blend their distinct styles and skills, resulting in innovative and diverse sounds that push the boundaries of lo-fi music. These joint efforts often lead to unique albums that capture the essence of multiple creative minds working together.

One notable example is the rise of collaborative compilations on platforms like Bandcamp, where various artists contribute tracks to a single project, showcasing a wide range of styles and influences. These compilations not only highlight individual talents but also promote a sense of unity and mutual support within the lo-fi community. By working together, artists can pool their resources and fanbases, achieving greater visibility and impact than they might on their own.

Challenges Facing the Lo-fi Community

One of the primary obstacles facing the growth and sustainability of the lo-fi music community is copyright and sampling constraints. Lo-fi music often incorporates samples from older records, movies, or other media to create its nostalgic and comforting soundscapes. However, obtaining legal clearance for these samples can be an expensive process. Many artists, especially those who are just starting out, may lack the resources or knowledge to navigate this complex legal landscape, leading to potential legal disputes and financial burdens.

Stricter copyright regulations pose significant implications for the sampling practices prevalent in lo-fi production. As governments around the world tighten intellectual property laws, lo-fi artists might find it increasingly challenging to use samples without facing legal consequences. This could stifle creativity as producers might shy away from using unique samples that give lo-fi music its distinctive charm. This means the genre could see a shift towards more original compositions, which may alter its fundamental aesthetic and appeal.

To address these challenges, artists and industry stakeholders are increasingly calling for clearer guidelines and, importantly, more accessible licensing options for sampling. Organizations dedicated to musicians' rights are pushing for reform in copyright laws to make them more favorable for creative expression. Educational programs and resources can also empower artists with the knowledge they need to navigate copyright issues effectively. By fostering a supportive and informed community, these initiatives can help maintain the genre's vibrancy.

Monetization and financial sustainability are pressing concerns for many lo-fi artists. Unlike mainstream genres, lo-fi music often struggles to generate substantial revenue due to its niche audience and the predominantly free distribution model on streaming platforms. Artists frequently earn minimal income from streams, making it difficult to sustain their careers solely through their music. This financial strain can deter new talent from entering the scene and limit the growth of existing artists.

The impact of streaming platforms and digital distribution on lo-fi artist compensation can't be overlooked. While these platforms provide global reach and accessibility, the royalties paid per stream are usually very low. This system disproportionately affects independent artists who rely heavily on streaming income. Some lo-fi creators turn to alternative revenue sources like merchandise sales, live performances, and fan support via crowdfunding platforms. However, these methods also present challenges, including the need for effective marketing and audience engagement strategies.

Exploring alternative revenue sources and creative strategies is crucial for sustaining a lo-fi music career. However, diversifying income streams by offering exclusive content and personalized experiences and leveraging social media for direct fan interaction can provide a more stable financial footing. Some artists have successfully turned to platforms like Patreon, where fans can support their favorite creators through monthly subscriptions. Developing a strong online presence and building a loyal fanbase are pivotal strategies in ensuring long-term sustainability in the lo-fi music scene.

Key Takeaways

- Technological advancements like AI and VR are transforming the lo-fi music scene.
- AI can streamline music production, but it raises questions about the authenticity of AI-generated lo-fi tracks.
- VR has the potential to create immersive lo-fi listening experiences and facilitate global virtual concerts.
- Hybridization with other genres and experimental techniques is making Lo-fi more versatile and innovative.
- Online platforms are fostering creativity and collaboration among emerging lo-fi artists, diversifying the genre.
- Copyright and sampling constraints pose challenges for lo-fi artists, requiring advocacy and education efforts.
- Monetization remains a pressing concern, with lo-fi artists needing to explore alternative revenue sources.
- The future of lo-fi music holds both promising opportunities and complex challenges that the community must navigate.
- Staying engaged, open-minded, and supportive will be crucial for the continued evolution and growth of the lo-fi scene.

Chapter 8

Appreciating the Aesthetics and Philosophy of Lo-fi Music

When you get to know more about lo-fi music, one of the first things you start to appreciate is how the genre celebrates imperfections as essential elements that define its unique character. Those so-called "flaws"—the hiss of tape, the crackle of vinyl, the slightly off-kilter notes—are not seen as things to be polished away but as integral parts of the sound that give Lo-fi its distinct charm.

It's a refreshing contrast to the pristine, hyper-produced tracks that dominate much mainstream music these days. In the lo-fi scene, there's this acknowledgment that perfection isn't the end goal—authenticity and emotional resonance are what really matter. And it's those little quirks and idiosyncrasies that make the music feel so much more alive, human, and relatable.

Take the way a lo-fi producer might deliberately distort a sample or manipulate the playback speed of a tape recorder. Rather than striving for technical flawlessness, they're embracing those unintended, "imperfect" textures as a means of imbuing the track with personality and depth. It's about prioritizing feel over clinical precision, creating a sonic landscape that pulls you in and makes you feel something.

It's not just the production techniques that celebrate imperfection—the entire lo-fi ethos is infused with this appreciation for the unpolished and the unconventional. Whether it's the way the artists approach song-writing, the gear they use, or the overall aesthetic they cultivate, there's this underlying message that perfection is overrated, and that beauty often lies in the little flaws.

For many lo-fi fans, this philosophy hits home on a really profound level. In a world that's increasingly obsessed with digital perfection, the genre provides a refreshing antidote—a reminder that the most captivating, emotionally resonant art is often the stuff that wears its heart on its sleeve. It's music that isn't afraid to be rough around the edges, to show its scars and blemishes, because that's where the real magic lies.

So, when you're listening to Lo-fi, try to tune into those imperfections and really appreciate them for what they are. The way the drums flutter and crackle, the slight warble in the melody, the ambient hiss that permeates the whole track—these aren't flaws to be fixed but integral parts of the lo-fi experience. They're what gives the music its soul, its personality, and its ability to transport you to another time and place.

It's a mindset that extends far beyond just the musical realm, too. The lo-fi ethos is really about celebrating the beauty in the unpolished, the unfinished, the imperfect—and recognizing that perfection is often overrated. Next time you find yourself getting caught up in the pursuit of pristine, flawless anything, remember the lesson of Lo-fi: sometimes, the most meaningful things in life are the ones that wear their scars with pride.

Understanding the Beauty in Imperfections

In the world of lo-fi music, imperfections are not just byproducts of the creative process; they are intentional stylistic choices that define the genre. Crackles from vinyl records, tape hisses, and even environmental noises like distant traffic or bird chirps are embedded within tracks to create a unique listening experience. These imperfections give lo-fi music its signature warmth and nostalgic feel, setting it apart from the polished productions of other genres.

Listeners often find these flaws endearing because they add an element of authenticity to the music. The subtle hiss of a tape or the occasional pop of a vinyl record can evoke memories and emotions, making the listening experience more personal and engaging. It's as if the music carries a piece of history with it, reminding listeners of simpler times and evoking a sense of comfort and familiarity.

Artists in the Lo-fi genre—incorporate these imperfections to enrich their soundscapes. They manipulate production techniques to include elements that most producers would typically edit out. This deliberate inclusion of "flaws" serves to humanize the music, making it feel handcrafted and intimate rather than sterile and mechanical. Such choices allow artists to create a distinct auditory signature that resonates deeply with their audience.

Historical Context of Imperfections

It's fascinating to see how the appreciation for imperfections has evolved in the world of lo-fi music. Back in the day, a lot of those "flaws" in the sound—the tape hiss, the vinyl crackle, the ever-so-slight timing issues—were just natural byproducts of the limited recording equipment available at the time. Over time, as technology advanced and music production became more polished, something interesting happened: a lot of artists started to really miss those analog quirks.

The truth is those imperfections didn't just add character to the music—they were an integral part of the emotional experience. When you heard that subtle background noise or that slightly off-kilter rhythm, it just made the whole thing feel so much rawer and more authentic. It was like you were getting a direct window into the artist's creative process, with all the little idiosyncrasies and humanity that come with it.

Nowadays, modern lo-fi producers are going out of their way to recreate those analog flaws using digital tools. They're sampling old tape recordings, manipulating playback speeds, and even adding in artificial crackles and hiss to capture that signature lo-fi vibe. The reason they do it is simple: those imperfections are just as essential to the lo-fi experience as the actual melodies and beats.

Think about it: when you hear that rain sound or that rustling of leaves woven into a lo-fi track, it's not just decorative background noise. It can actually transform the entire emotional landscape of the music, evoking feelings of peace, introspection, and connection. Those little "flaws" become expressive tools that allow artists to tap into a whole new realm of meaning and authenticity.

That's the real power of imperfections in Lo-fi—they give the music this innate human quality that you just can't replicate with clinical, hyper-polished production. It's about embracing the quirks and idiosyncrasies and using them to create something that feels so much more real, so much more relatable. It's music that wears its heart on its sleeve, unafraid to show its scars and blemishes.

So, when you're listening to lo-fi, try to really tune into those little imperfections. Notice how they shape the emotional landscape of the track, how they transform the ordinary into the poignant. Those so-called "flaws" are what make lo-fi music so captivating, so powerful, and so profoundly, authentically human.

Embracing Minimalist Production

One of the most captivating aspects of lo-fi music lies in its embrace of simplicity and minimalism. The philosophy of "less is more" is a core tenet that contributes to the genre's charm and depth. In Lo-fi, minimalist production allows for an intense focus on essential elements such as melody and atmosphere. By stripping down to these basic components, artists can create tracks that are profound and serene without overwhelming the listener with excessive sounds and effects.

Simplicity in lo-fi music ensures that each element present has a purpose and a place. This approach creates a clean soundscape where melodies can breathe, and atmospheres can flourish. Rather than cramming numerous layers into a track, lo-fi artists often opt for sparse arrangements, allowing each note and beat to resonate meaningfully. This deliberate restraint fosters an intimate listening experience, where the subtleties of the music come to the forefront, inviting listeners to engage more deeply with the sound.

For example, in many lo-fi tracks, the use of gentle piano lines or soft guitar riffs set a mellow tone, accompanied by subdued rhythmic patterns. These elements, though simple, work together to create a cohesive and immersive auditory environment. The minimalistic approach encourages listeners to focus on the emotional and atmospheric qualities of the music.

The impact of space and silence in lo-fi music cannot be understated. Silence, when used effectively, becomes a powerful tool that shapes the overall mood of a track. Lo-fi artists often incorporate pauses and gaps within their compositions, creating a breathing space that enhances the emotional depth of the music. These moments of silence allow listeners to reflect and absorb the nuances of the track, making the listening experience more personal and contemplative.

Space in lo-fi music operates similarly, providing room for each sound to exist without competition. This method not only emphasizes individual elements but also contributes to a relaxed and introspective atmosphere. When there is ample space between notes and beats, the listener's mind has the opportunity to wander and explore the textures and layers of the music at a leisurely pace. Such an environment is conducive to relaxation and reflection, key attributes of the Lo-fi genre.

The strategic use of space and silence aligns with the genre's ethos of minimalism. It strips away any unnecessary clutter, allowing the core components of the track to shine. By doing so, lo-fi artists can create music that feels both spacious and intimate, striking a delicate balance that resonates with listeners on a profound level.

Another hallmark of lo-fi music is simplicity in arrangements. Lo-fi artists adeptly utilize straightforward musical structures to convey complex emotions and themes. The beauty of this lies in the ability to evoke strong feelings through unadorned and direct means.

Consider how a simple chord progression, when paired with subtle embellishments like light percussion or ambient sounds, can evoke a sense of nostalgia or melancholy. These uncomplicated arrangements tap into universal emotions, making the music relatable and poignant. By focusing on fundamental musical ideas, lo-fi artists can communicate intricate emotional landscapes without relying on elaborate compositions.

Moreover, this simplicity lends itself to versatility and accessibility.

Lo-fi tracks can easily adapt to various contexts, whether it's background music for studying or a soundtrack for winding down after a long day. The straightforward nature of the arrangements ensures that the music remains unobtrusive while still being evocative and engaging.

When comparing lo-fi music with more complexly produced genres, the unique appeal of minimalism becomes even more apparent. While genres like electronic dance music or progressive rock might rely on densely layered tracks and intricate arrangements, Lo-fi stands out by embracing a pared-down aesthetic.

Supporting Independent Lo-fi Artists

Supporting independent lo-fi artists is crucial for nurturing a vibrant and diverse music community. When fans rally behind these artists, it really does make a world of difference. It's not just about the music itself—it's about contributing to this thriving ecosystem where creativity and authenticity can truly flourish.

Think about it—when you attend a local lo-fi show, purchase albums directly from the artists, or share their work on social media, you're not just passively consuming the music. You're actively participating in the growth and sustainability of the entire genre. You're helping these independent musicians feel valued, supported, and motivated to keep pushing the boundaries of their craft.

The collaborative spirit within the lo-fi community is another big part of what makes it so special. These artists aren't just competing against each other—they're constantly joining forces, sharing resources, and cross-pollinating ideas. It's in those collaborative efforts that we often see the most innovative, genre-blending tracks emerge. That diversity and creative synergy is what gives Lo-fi its richness and depth.

Fan engagement goes way beyond just music consumption. When listeners start actively participating in online forums, sharing playlists, and providing feedback, they're helping cultivate this tight-knit, supportive community that extends far beyond the music itself. That sense of belonging and shared appreciation keeps both artists and fans dedicated to the genre, ensuring its continued growth and evolution.

And you know, a big part of what makes independent lo-fi artists so compelling is the artistic freedom they get to enjoy. Without the constraints of major labels or commercial pressures, they can really lean into their experimental side, blending genres, exploring personal themes, and constantly pushing the boundaries of what's possible. That kind of unrestricted creativity is where the most exciting, boundary-pushing music comes from.

Creative freedom doesn't just benefit the artists—it also creates a culture of authenticity that resonates deeply with listeners. When musicians are free to express their true selves and share their unfiltered perspectives, it builds an incredibly strong connection between the art and the audience. You're not just listening to some generic, focus-grouped track—you're connecting with the artist's unique voice and lived experiences.

The DIY ethos that's so central to lo-fi culture plays a big role in preserving that authenticity. When artists are hands-on with every aspect of their work, from composition to distribution, the end result is a pure reflection of their original vision. There's no outside influence diluting or compromising the music—it's just the artist, their craft, and their connection with the audience.

Of course, financial stability is crucial for independent lo-fi musicians to keep doing what they love. That's where direct fan support, through platforms like Bandcamp and Patreon, becomes so invaluable. When listeners invest in the artists, they love by purchasing music, merch, and tickets, it ensures that these creators can maintain their independence and keep innovating.

So, in the end, supporting independent lo-fi artists isn't just about enjoying great music—it's about nurturing a vibrant, diverse, and authentic community that celebrates creativity in all its forms. Whether you're attending shows, sharing playlists, or contributing directly to your favorite musicians, your involvement is what keeps this whole ecosystem thriving. For lo-fi fans, that's a pretty incredible thing to be a part of.

Key Takeaways

- Appreciation for the unique appeal of lo-fi music and its embrace of imperfections.
- Vinyl crackles, tape hisses, and other "flaws" are deliberate choices that create a comforting, authentic, and personal listening experience.
- Lo-fi music is an art form that speaks volumes with its simplicity and rawness, offering a profound sense of peace and introspection.
- The use of digital tools to mimic analog sounds is a nod to the past, blending old and new to keep the spirit of Lo-fi alive.
- Lo-fi music fosters a community of independent artists, encouraging creativity and collaboration, and ensuring the genre's evolution.
- Embracing the imperfections and minimalist philosophy of Lo-fi could lead to a more authentic, connected, and serene existence.

- Tuning into lo-fi music allows one to get lost in its gentle hums and subtle rhythms, offering a unique and transformative experience.

Chapter 9

Key Artists Shaping the Lo-fi Music Landscape

Lo-fi music has always been about more than just the production techniques or the signature lo-fi aesthetic. At its core, it's a genre driven by the innovative visions and creative spirits of the musicians who have devoted themselves to perfecting this unique sound. From the pioneering producers who laid the groundwork to the contemporary innovators constantly pushing the boundaries, these lo-fi artists have left an indelible mark, not just on the music itself, but on the passionate community of fans that has grown alongside it.

By understanding the rich histories and creative journeys of these lo-fi trailblazers, we can gain a deeper appreciation for the artistic depth and versatility that define this ever-evolving genre.

We'll look not only at the work of the pioneering icons of the past—we'll also delve into the work of contemporary lo-fi luminaries who are continuing to push the genre in bold, unexpected directions. Artists like Knxwledge, with his kaleidoscopic, genre-blending compositions, and the collaborative collectives like Chillhop, who have played a pivotal role in elevating emerging lo-fi talents—these are the visionaries whose imprint can be felt across the ever-evolving lo-fi landscape.

By unpacking the stories and artistic approaches of these lo-fi trailblazers, we'll gain a richer understanding of the genre's foundations, its defining characteristics, and the myriad ways in which it has evolved over time. Whether it's the meticulous sampling techniques, the embrace of imperfection, or the seamless integration of diverse cultural influences, the creative brilliance of these lo-fi icons has left an indelible mark, inspiring countless others to pick up the torch and continue pushing the boundaries of what's possible within this remarkable artform.

Profiles of Pioneering Artists

At the heart of the Lo-fi movement are the artists whose visionary work has defined the genre's distinct character. These pioneers have not only honed their craft but have also imbued their music with a deep sense of authenticity and emotional resonance, setting the stage for future generations of lo-fi musicians to build upon.

The Legacy of Nujabes

One such artist is Nujabes, the late Japanese producer whose atmospheric, jazz-infused lo-fi compositions have captivated audiences worldwide. Nujabes' unique sound was a testament to his eclectic musical influences, blending elements of hip-hop, ambient, and traditional Japanese instrumentation to create a lush, contemplative listening experience.

What made Nujabes' approach so groundbreaking was his unwavering commitment to authenticity and attention to detail. Instead of relying on overly polished production techniques, he embraced the warmth and imperfections of analog gear, purposefully incorporating subtle tape hiss, vinyl crackle, and other lo-fi textures into his tracks. This intentional use of "flaws" imbued his music with a timeless, nostalgic quality that resonated deeply with listeners.

But Nujabes' impact extended far beyond just his sonic signature. His music also served as a vehicle for profound emotional expression, with tracks like "Luv(sic)" and "Feather" exploring themes of loss, introspection, and the human condition. By seamlessly weaving these weighty ideas into his compositions, Nujabes elevated Lo-fi beyond just a production style, transforming it into a powerful medium for storytelling and personal reflection.

The legacy of Nujabes can be heard echoing through the work of countless contemporary lo-fi artists, who have drawn inspiration from his pioneering spirit and innovative approach. Producers like Shing02 and Uyama Hiroto, both of whom collaborated extensively with Nujabes, have continued to build upon his musical foundations, further expanding the sonic and thematic possibilities of the genre.

These formative experiences have clearly left an indelible mark, as Shing02 and Uyama Hiroto have gone on to craft their own distinctive lo-fi soundscapes that pay homage to Nujabes' trailblazing spirit while also pushing the genre in bold new directions.

For Shing02, his work with Nujabes on seminal tracks like "Luv(sic)" showcased a seamless synthesis of Nujabes' atmospheric, jazz-inflected production and Shing02's evocative lyrical storytelling. Building upon this collaborative foundation, Shing02 has continued to explore themes of loss, contemplation, and the human condition through his solo lo-fi compositions, imbuing them with a depth and emotional resonance that honors Nujabes' own penchant for using music as a vehicle for profound self-expression.

In Shing02's hands, the lo-fi aesthetic becomes a canvas for poetic reflection, as heard in tracks like "Reflection Eternal" and "Peaceland." Here, the warm, hazy textures and subdued rhythms create a sonic environment that perfectly complements the artist's introspective lyrics, inviting the listener to get lost in the meditative, almost trance-like qualities of the music.

Meanwhile, Uyama Hiroto has carved out his own distinct niche within the lo-fi sphere, leveraging his extensive knowledge of jazz and classical music to craft compositions that both pay homage to Nujabes' sound while also infusing it with new levels of harmonic sophistication and melodic complexity.

Tracks like "Far Flowers" and "Aruarian Dance" showcase Uyama Hiroto's virtuosic approach, blending lush, atmospheric pads with intricate, jazz-inflected chord progressions and delicate, almost cinematic flourishes. The result is a sound that feels both familiar and entirely fresh, with Uyama Hiroto seamlessly weaving together Nujabes' signature lo-fi textures with his own unique musical sensibilities.

However, the influence of Nujabes extends beyond just the sonic realm; both Shing02 and Uyama Hiroto have also carried on the master producer's penchant for using lo-fi music as a medium for deeper artistic expression. Like Nujabes, they've imbued their compositions with a sense of emotional resonance and conceptual weight, exploring themes of introspection, solitude, and the human experience through their evocative, immersive soundscapes.

In this way, Shing02 and Uyama Hiroto have not only honored Nujabes' legacy as a pioneering lo-fi artist but have also helped to expand the thematic and creative possibilities of the genre as a whole. By building upon the foundations laid by their mentor, they've demonstrated the limitless potential of lo-fi music to serve as a vehicle for profound personal and artistic exploration—a testament to the enduring power and influence of Nujabes' visionary work.

DJ Shadow's Legacy

Another lo-fi luminary who has left an indelible mark on the community is DJ Shadow. He is known for his experimental use of sampling. DJ Shadow's Landmark Album *Endtroducing.....* is widely regarded as a seminal work in the history of lo-fi music. By meticulously repurposing obscure records and crafting dense, collage-like tracks, he demonstrated the boundless potential of sample-based production.

What made DJ Shadow's approach so revolutionary was his ability to imbue his music with layers of meaning and emotion. Each sample he utilized became a building block in a larger mosaic, contributing to a soundscape rich in detail and texture. This technique allowed him to transcend the limitations of traditional genre boundaries, creating something truly unique and genre-defying.

DJ Shadow's influence can be felt far beyond his discography, as his pioneering work paved the way for other producers to adopt a more holistic and exploratory approach to music-making. Today, many lo-fi artists draw direct inspiration from his methods, incorporating diverse samples and unconventional structures into their own compositions. His trailblazing efforts have served as a testament to the power of sampling, encouraging a new generation of musicians to push the boundaries of the genre further.

Alongside these groundbreaking producers, the lo-fi scene has also been shaped by the distinctive voices of individual artists who have used the genre as a platform for personal expression. One such figure is J Dilla, the late Detroit-based musician whose raw, emotive production style has become a touchstone for lo-fi enthusiasts.

What set J Dilla apart was his unwavering embrace of imperfection. Rather than striving for clinical precision, he celebrated the inherent flaws and quirks of his homemade production techniques, manipulating analog gear to achieve a sound that was both gritty and heartfelt. This approach, which stood in stark contrast to the hyper-polished productions that were becoming increasingly prevalent, resonated deeply with listeners who craved a more authentic, human-centric listening experience.

Beyond his signature sound, J Dilla's impact on the Lo-fi genre can be attributed to his relentless creativity and singular artistic vision. He was never content to simply replicate a formula, constantly pushing the boundaries of what was possible within the confines of lo-fi production. His collaborations with a diverse array of artists, from rappers to jazz musicians, further cemented his status as a true innovator, blurring the lines between genres and forging new sonic pathways.

The legacy of J Dilla can be felt across the lo-fi landscape, with countless producers emulating his distinctive style and techniques. His willingness to embrace imperfection and prioritize emotional resonance over technical prowess has inspired a new generation of musicians to approach their craft with a similar sense of fearlessness and authenticity.

Case Studies of Iconic Artists

To truly appreciate the breadth and depth of lo-fi music, one needs to delve deeper into the stories and creative journeys of some of the genre's most iconic artists. By examining their unique approaches, cultural inspirations, and lasting impacts, we can gain a richer understanding of the multifaceted nature of this ever-evolving genre.

Knxwledge

One such artist is the enigmatic Knxwledge, whose prolific output and boundary-pushing sound have cemented his status as a lo-fi trailblazer. Hailing from Los Angeles, Knxwledge's compositions are a mesmerizing blend of dusty samples, hazy atmospherics, and intricate rhythmic patterns—a sonic tapestry that seamlessly integrates elements of hip-hop, soul, and, of course, the signature lo-fi aesthetic.

What sets Knxwledge apart is his unapologetically experimental approach to music-making. He's not content to simply recreate the traditional lo-fi sound. Instead, he's constantly pushing the boundaries, incorporating unexpected textures, unconventional structures, and avant-garde production techniques into his work. This relentless drive to innovate has resulted in a vast and diverse discography, encompassing everything from beat tapes to collaborative albums with acclaimed artists like Anderson.Paak.

But Knxwledge's impact extends far beyond just his own creative output. As the founder of the acclaimed record label Stones Throw, he's played a pivotal role in nurturing and elevating the work of other lo-fi visionaries, providing them with a platform to share their unique artistic visions. This collaborative spirit, coupled with Knxwledge's own boundary-pushing sensibilities, has helped shape the broader lo-fi landscape, inspiring a new generation of producers to embrace their inner eccentricities and forge their own distinct sonic paths.

Chillhop

Another lo-fi luminary whose influence can't be overstated is Chillhop, the collective responsible for curating some of the genre's most iconic and widely recognized playlists. What started as a humble YouTube channel has evolved into a multifaceted creative enterprise, encompassing not just music curation but also visual art, merchandise, and even live events.

At the heart of Chillhop's success is their unwavering dedication to discovering and championing emerging lo-fi talents from around the world. Through their meticulously curated playlists, they've introduced countless listeners to a diverse array of artists, each with their own unique sonic signatures and thematic explorations. This commitment to showcasing the genre's breadth and versatility has been instrumental in fueling the growth and mainstream acceptance of lo-fi music.

Chillhop's impact extends beyond just curation; they've also played a pivotal role in fostering a tight-knit community of lo-fi enthusiasts. Through their online platforms, social media channels, and live events, they've cultivated a space where fans and artists can connect, share their passions, and collectively celebrate the genre's enduring appeal. This sense of camaraderie and mutual appreciation has been a driving force in the lo-fi scene, inspiring collaborations, cross-pollination of ideas, and a shared dedication to elevating the art form.

As Lo-fi continues to evolve and captivate audiences worldwide, the influence of artists like Knxwledge and the Chillhop collective will undoubtedly continue to reverberate. Their pioneering spirit, unwavering commitment to artistic integrity, and ability to nurture and amplify new voices have cemented their status as essential pillars of the lo-fi music community.

Influences of Modern Lo-fi Musicians

The lo-fi genre has always been characterized by its eclectic and ever-evolving nature, with successive generations of artists building upon the foundations laid by their predecessors. As the contemporary lo-fi landscape expands, we've witnessed a flourishing of creative cross-pollination, where musicians are fearlessly blending traditional lo-fi elements with a diverse array of influences, pushing the boundaries of what the genre can be.

One of the most compelling aspects of modern lo-fi music is the way it seamlessly integrates elements from a wide range of musical styles and cultural traditions. Artists like Knxwledge, as we've previously discussed, have made a name for themselves by crafting compositions that defy easy categorization, drawing inspiration from the expansive realms of hip-hop, soul, jazz, and beyond.

Ohbliv

Ohbliv is a Japanese lo-fi producer whose music is a mesmerizing fusion of classic lo-fi sounds and traditional Japanese influences. When you listen to his tracks, it's like being transported to this enchanting realm where the familiar and the exotic come together in perfect harmony.

Ohbliv's productions, on the one hand, are steeped in the warm, hazy, lo-fi aesthetic we all know and love. You've got those soothing, atmospheric textures, subtle crackles, and pops that give the music an organic, handcrafted feel. It's the kind of sound that just wraps listeners in a cozy, nostalgic embrace, making you feel like you're listening to a lost treasure from the past.

Ohbliv seamlessly weaves in these captivating elements of traditional Japanese music—the delicate, almost hypnotic rhythms and the delicate melodies that seem to float through the mix. It's like he's taking these familiar lo-fi tropes and infusing them with a whole other layer of cultural richness and sonic complexity.

The result is an utterly transformative listening experience. One moment, you're immersed in these beautifully melancholic, lo-fi vibes. The next, you're transported to this serene, almost otherworldly realm, where the boundaries between the modern and the ancient blur together into this mesmerizing sonic tapestry.

It's the kind of music that really engages all your senses, enveloping you in a sensory experience that is both comfortingly familiar and thrillingly novel. You can't help but get caught up in the ebb and flow of those hypnotic rhythms, the delicate interplay between the organic lo-fi textures and the traditional Japanese instrumentation.

What's so special about Ohbliv's approach is the way he maintains this perfect balance between the two distinct musical worlds. He's not just mashing them together haphazardly—there's intentionality and artistry to the way he blends these elements, creating something that feels cohesive and wholly unique.

It's the kind of music that really taps into the innate human desire to explore, seek out new cultural horizons, and discover the beauty in the unfamiliar. By bringing these two rich musical traditions together in such a seamless, captivating way, Ohbliv has crafted a sound that transcends boundaries and speaks to the universal language of emotion and atmospherics.

Bossa Nova Beats

We've seen lo-fi artists from Latin America, such as the Brazilian collective Bossa Nova Beats, incorporate the lush, melodic sensibilities of bossa nova and samba into their lo-fi compositions. The interplay between the genre's signature atmospheric qualities and the rhythmic sophistication of these Latin American influences has given rise to a truly unique and captivating subgenre of lo-fi music.

The cross-pollination of Lo-fi isn't limited to just geographical or cultural boundaries. Contemporary musicians are also actively exploring the intersections between Lo-fi and other established genres, fusing the genre's mellow, nostalgic vibe with the energy and dynamism of styles like indie rock, electronic, and even classical music.

Take, for example, the work of lo-fi artist Chet Baker, whose compositions seamlessly blend the intimate lo-fi aesthetic with the elegant, jazz-infused sensibilities of his namesake, the legendary trumpeter. The result is a sound that is both deeply rooted in tradition and refreshingly innovative, captivating listeners with its blend of lo-fi textures and refined musicality.

Another artist who has pushed the boundaries of Lo-fi is Japanese producer Joji, whose work has drawn from the realms of alternative R&B and lo-fi pop. Tracks like "Slow Dancing in the Dark" showcase Joji's ability to craft emotionally resonant, atmospheric compositions that resonate with a wide range of listeners. They simultaneously honor the genre's heritage and usher in a new era of cross-pollination.

These modern lo-fi innovators aren't just passively drawing from other genres; they're actively reinterpreting and reimagining the very essence of what Lo-fi can be. By incorporating diverse influences and techniques, they're expanding the sonic and thematic possibilities of the genre, ensuring that it remains a vital, ever-evolving art form that continues to captivate and inspire music enthusiasts worldwide.

Sampling Techniques in Contemporary Lo-fi Music

At the heart of lo-fi music's creative ethos lies the art of sampling—the thoughtful and innovative repurposing of existing sounds and recordings to craft new, evocative compositions. As the genre has evolved, contemporary lo-fi artists have elevated sampling from a mere production tool to a powerful means of artistic expression, using it to imbue their music with deeper layers of meaning and cultural resonance.

One of the most compelling aspects of sampling in modern Lo-fi is the way artists carefully curate and recontextualize their source material. Rather than simply extracting random sounds or beats, lo-fi producers approach the sampling process with reverence for the original work. They carefully select and manipulate these elements, creating something that pays homage to the past while still feeling refreshingly new and innovative.

Take, for instance, the work of Ohbliv, the Japanese lo-fi artist we touched on earlier. In tracks like "Dusk Till Dawn," Ohbliv masterfully weaves together fragments of traditional Japanese instrumentation with hazy, atmospheric, lo-fi textures, crafting a mesmerizing soundscape that transports the listener to a dreamlike, culturally infused realm. By thoughtfully integrating these cultural signifiers into his compositions, Ohbliv not only pays respect to his musical heritage but also imbues his work with a profound sense of identity and place.

Similarly, lo-fi artists like Knxwledge and Madlib have built their reputations on their virtuosic sampling abilities, demonstrating a keen eye for unearthing obscure musical gems and repurposing them in innovative ways. Whether it's the way Knxwledge transforms a forgotten soul recording into a hypnotic, head-nodding beat or Madlib's ability to seamlessly blend disparate musical elements into a cohesive whole, these producers have elevated sampling to an art form, using it as a means of archiving and reinterpreting musical history.

However, the creative power of sampling in contemporary Lo-fi extends beyond just the production process. Many artists have also recognized the importance of originality and authenticity in their sampling-based compositions, actively striving to imbue their work with a distinctive, personal touch that sets them apart from their peers.

Take, for example, the work of the lo-fi artist bsd.u, whose track

"Numb" deftly incorporates elements of vintage drum machine recordings and hazy atmospheric pads, weaving them together into a captivating, emotionally charged composition. What sets bsd.u's approach apart is the way he molds these sampled elements into something that feels uniquely his own, blending them with his own original melodies and rhythmic structures to create a track that is both deeply rooted in the past and firmly grounded in the present.

This emphasis on originality and personal expression is crucial in the contemporary lo-fi landscape, where the sheer volume of sampling-based music can sometimes lead to concerns about creative stagnation or unoriginal pastiche. By constantly pushing the boundaries of what's possible with sampling, lo-fi artists are ensuring that the genre remains a vibrant, ever-evolving art form, one that continues to captivate and inspire listeners with its boundless creativity and innovative spirit.

Collaborations Within the Lo-fi Community

One of the most defining characteristics of the lo-fi music scene is its collaborative spirit, where artists from diverse backgrounds come together to cross-pollinate ideas, share resources, and collectively elevate the genre. Whether it's through virtual partnerships forged over the internet or synergistic relationships cultivated within independent labels, the lo-fi community has fostered a culture of mutual support and creative synergy that has been instrumental in its ongoing evolution.

The rise of digital platforms has been a key driver in facilitating these collaborative efforts within the lo-fi realm. Websites like Bandcamp and SoundCloud, as well as social media channels, have provided artists with accessible, user-friendly tools to connect, share their work, and engage in creative exchanges that transcend geographical boundaries.

Take, for instance, the work of the lo-fi collective, "Sleepy Fish," which has leveraged the power of online collaboration to craft a series of acclaimed compilation albums. By inviting a diverse array of lo-fi producers to contribute original tracks, the collective has not only showcased the breadth of talent within the genre but has also fostered a sense of community and mutual appreciation among its members.

Through these collaborative projects, lo-fi artists have been able to learn from one another, sharing production techniques, sample sources, and creative approaches that have ultimately enriched the sonic landscape of the genre. Moreover, the exposure gained from appearing on these high-profile compilations has helped to elevate the profiles of emerging artists, introducing their work to new audiences and expanding their creative and professional opportunities.

The collaborative spirit of the lo-fi scene extends beyond just virtual partnerships. Many artists have also found success by aligning themselves with independent, artist-run labels that have become vital hubs of support and creative expression within the genre.

Labels like Chillhop Music and Tru Thoughts, for example, have not only provided lo-fi musicians with the resources and platforms to showcase their work but have also cultivated a sense of artistic community that has been crucial in nurturing the growth and evolution of the genre. These labels often operate on principles of mutual support, encouraging their artists to engage in cross-pollination and joint projects that further strengthen the bonds within the lo-fi ecosystem.

One such example is the recent collaboration between lo-fi artists Edamame and Philanthrope, who teamed up to release the acclaimed album "Crossroads" on the Tru Thoughts label. By combining their distinctive production styles and creative visions, the two artists crafted a work that was greater than the sum of its parts, showcasing the power of collaboration to push the boundaries of what lo-fi music can achieve.

Key Takeaways

- Pioneering lo-fi artists like Nujabes, Shing02, Uyama Hiroto, DJ Shadow, and J Dilla have left an indelible mark on the genre through their unique styles, innovative approaches, and profound emotional resonance.
- Case studies of iconic lo-fi artists, such as the experimental producer Knxwledge and the influential Chillhop collective, underscore their significant contributions to shaping the lo-fi landscape.
- Modern lo-fi music reflects a flourishing of creative cross-pollination, as artists integrate diverse cultural elements, fuse lo-fi with other genres, and utilize innovative sampling techniques to imbue their work with deeper meaning and personal expression.
- The collaborative spirit within the lo-fi community is a defining characteristic facilitated by online platforms and artist-run labels that foster connections, support emerging talents, and showcase the genre's diversity through joint projects and compilations.
- Across the chapter, the emphasis is on understanding the rich histories, creative visions, and lasting impacts of the pioneering and contemporary lo-fi artists who have continuously elevated and expanded the genre.

Chapter 10

The Cultural Impact of Lo-fi Music

In the ever-evolving landscape of music, certain genres transcend their artistic boundaries and become woven into the very fabric of our cultural tapestry. Lo-fi music is one such genre, captivating audiences worldwide with its distinctive sound, emotive resonance, and ability to shape societal trends. From its presence in mainstream media to its role as a tool for relaxation and productivity, Lo-fi's influence has permeated deep into the collective consciousness, leaving an indelible mark on the way we experience and engage with music.

By understanding the diverse ways in which Lo-fi has left its imprint, we can gain a greater appreciation for the genre's significance and its ability to touch the lives of people from all walks of life.

Lo-fi Music in Mainstream Media

One of the most tangible indicators of Lo-fi's cultural impact is its growing presence in mainstream media. From being featured in popular TV shows and commercials to serving as the soundtrack for blockbuster films, Lo-fi's soothing, atmospheric qualities have made it an increasingly sought-after musical element in popular culture.

Take, for instance, the use of lo-fi tracks in hit series like *Euphoria* and

Stranger Things. The producers of these shows have masterfully incorporated Lo-fi's warm, hazy textures to enhance the emotional resonance of crucial scenes, whether it's a contemplative moment of introspection or a montage that captures the nostalgia of a bygone era. By weaving these lo-fi sounds into the fabric of the narrative, they've not only elevated the viewing experience but have also introduced the genre to a broader audience that may have previously been unfamiliar with its charms.

It's not only the realm of television that Lo-fi has made its mark. Brands from various industries have also recognized the power of these atmospheric soundscapes, using them in their advertising campaigns to evoke a sense of authenticity, calm, and connection with their target consumers. Whether it's a soothing lo-fi track playing in the background of a serene nature-inspired commercial or the inclusion of a lo-fi-infused track in a brand's social media content, the use of lo-fi music has become an increasingly common and effective way for companies to connect with their audience on a deeper, more emotive level.

The cultural impact of Lo-fi's mainstream presence extends beyond just its ability to enhance visuals and set the mood. The integration of lo-fi sounds into popular media has also helped to reshape broader musical trends, influencing the way audiences engage with and appreciate music as a whole.

As Lo-fi has gained more exposure and recognition, it's clear that listeners are growing increasingly interested in a minimalist, atmospheric approach to music-making. This shift reflects a broader cultural movement towards simplicity, authenticity, and a rejection of the overly polished, formulaic productions that have long dominated the mainstream. By embracing the imperfections and raw textures that define the lo-fi aesthetic, audiences are signaling a desire for a more genuine, emotionally resonant musical experience.

The collaborations between lo-fi artists and their mainstream counterparts have further amplified the genre's impact, introducing lo-fi sounds to new demographics and blurring the lines between underground and commercial music. These cross-pollinations not only expand the reach of Lo-fi but also contribute to the ongoing evolution of popular music as artists continue to explore the creative potential of blending lo-fi elements with more conventional production styles.

Lo-fi's increasing presence in mainstream media is a testament to the genre's growing cultural significance. By captivating audiences with its ability to evoke emotions, create atmospheric ambiance, and challenge prevailing musical norms, Lo-fi has solidified its place as a vital, ever-evolving force within the broader cultural landscape.

Lo-fi as a Study Aid and Relaxation Tool

Beyond its impact on mainstream media, lo-fi music has also carved out a unique niche for itself as a powerful tool for productivity, focus, and relaxation. Its calming, repetitive nature has made it an increasingly popular choice for those seeking a soothing sonic backdrop to enhance their daily routines and activities.

For many students and professionals, lo-fi playlists have become an indispensable part of their study and work environments. The gentle, unobtrusive beats and melodic loops inherent in lo-fi music have proven to be highly effective in creating a conducive atmosphere for concentration and focus. By providing a rhythmic foundation without distracting lyrics or sudden changes in dynamics, Lo-fi helps to maintain a steady, focused pace, allowing the listener to immerse themselves in their tasks without being pulled away by more attention-grabbing musical elements.

This practical application of Lo-fi as a study aid has not gone unnoticed, with countless online tutorials, articles, and even dedicated Lo-fi study playlists catering to the needs of individuals seeking to maximize their productivity and academic performance. The repetitive, calming nature of lo-fi tracks has been shown to enhance cognitive function, reduce stress, and foster a sense of tranquility—all of which are crucial ingredients for effective studying and task completion.

The benefits of Lo-fi's soothing qualities extend beyond just the academic or professional realm. The genre has also emerged as a popular tool for relaxation and stress management, with listeners turning to its gentle melodies and atmospheric textures to unwind and find a sense of inner peace.

In an age where the demands of modern life can often feel overwhelming, Lo-fi's ability to promote a state of calm and mindfulness has made it an increasingly valuable resource for those seeking respite from the stresses of daily existence. Whether it's the soft pitter-patter of rain samples layered over a mellow, contemplative beat or the warm, enveloping hum of vintage synthesizers, Lo-fi's sonic tapestry has a unique way of transporting the listener to a serene, meditative space—one where the worries and distractions of the outside world fade into the background.

As a result, Lo-fi has become a fixture in the wellness industry, with dedicated playlists, relaxation apps, and even sleep-focused audio tracks featuring its signature lo-fi sound. By tapping into the genre's inherent therapeutic qualities, these curated experiences not only provide a means of stress relief but also contribute to a broader cultural shift towards incorporating mindfulness and self-care practices into our daily lives.

Lo-fi's dual role as both a productivity-enhancing study aid and a soothing, relaxation-inducing tool speaks to the genre's versatility and its ability to cater to a wide range of human needs. Whether you're a student cramming for an exam or a busy professional seeking a moment of respite, Lo-fi's calming, atmospheric qualities can offer a welcome respite, helping to foster a healthier, more balanced approach to our daily routines and activities.

Lo-fi and Cultural Movements

As lo-fi music has gained widespread recognition and appreciation, it has also become inextricably linked to various cultural movements and ideologies that resonate with its underlying ethos and aesthetic. From its counter-cultural roots to its role in fostering a sense of community and inclusivity, Lo-fi's influence has extended far beyond the boundaries of the music industry, becoming a reflection of broader societal shifts and value systems.

At the heart of Lo-fi's cultural significance is its unwavering commitment to authenticity and artistic independence. The genre's DIY approach to production, which embraces imperfections and rejects the gloss of mainstream commercialism, aligns closely with the values espoused by many counter-cultural movements. This anti-establishment sensibility, coupled with Lo-fi's emphasis on individual expression and the celebration of the "underdog," has made it a natural ally for those who seek to challenge the status quo and forge their own creative paths.

This alignment with non-conformist ideals has not gone unnoticed, as Lo-fi's distinctive sound and visual aesthetic have become increasingly associated with various subcultures and artistic communities that prioritize authenticity, creativity, and a rejection of mainstream norms. Whether it's the lo-fi-infused chillwave scene, the resurgence of cassette tape culture, or the rise of bedroom producers and DIY record labels,

Lo-fi's influence can be seen woven throughout these movements, serving as a unifying sonic thread that connects like-minded individuals in their pursuit of artistic and personal freedom.

Lo-fi's cultural impact extends beyond just its counter-cultural associations. The genre has also played a significant role in fostering a sense of community and inclusivity among its devoted fanbase. Through the proliferation of online platforms, lo-fi enthusiasts from around the world have been able to connect, share their passion for lo-fi music, and engage in collaborative projects that transcend geographical boundaries.

These virtual spaces, be it dedicated Lo-fi subreddits, Discord servers, or YouTube channels, have become hubs of cultural exchange, where fans can not only discover new artists and tracks but also participate in discussions, share personal stories, and forge meaningful relationships with fellow lo-fi devotees. This sense of belonging and camaraderie, rooted in a shared appreciation for the genre's unique sonic qualities and underlying ethos, has helped to cultivate a global community of lo-fi enthusiasts who see the music as more than just a passive listening experience.

As Lo-fi continues to gain mainstream recognition and exposure, its ability to resonate with counter-cultural movements and foster a sense of global community will undoubtedly remain a crucial aspect of its cultural significance. Whether it inspires a new generation of DIY creatives or serves as a unifying force that connects music enthusiasts worldwide, Lo-fi's influence on the broader cultural landscape is a testament to the enduring power of authentic, artistic expression.

Key Takeaways

- Lo-fi music has transcended artistic boundaries to become woven into the cultural fabric, captivating global audiences.
- It has a growing presence in mainstream media, being used in TV, commercials, and films to enhance emotional resonance and ambiance.
- It has contributed to reshaping musical trends towards more minimalist, authentic experiences.
- Carved niche as a tool for productivity, focus, and relaxation, fostering conducive study/work environments.
- Its therapeutic qualities have led to widespread adoption in the wellness industry for promoting mindfulness and stress relief.
- Alignment with counter-cultural movements and emphasis on authenticity resonates with those challenging mainstream.
- The proliferation of online platforms enabled the global lo-fi community to connect, collaborate, and celebrate the genre.
- Universal themes, emotional resonance, and digital accessibility facilitated the cross-pollination of regional styles and influences.
- Lo-fi's cultural impact will continue to reverberate, influencing trends and inspiring cross-cultural collaboration.

Conclusion

As we conclude our journey through the fascinating world of lo-fi music, let's revisit some of the key points we've discussed. We delved into the historical roots and evolution of lo-fi music, tracing its origins from the early days of analog recording to the digital era that has made this genre widely accessible today. From cassette culture and DIY aesthetics to the widespread use of sampling and lo-fi production techniques, we've uncovered the nitty-gritty details that make lo-fi music unique.

We've also explored the essence of what makes Lo-fi so captivating—its chill vibes, relaxed beats, and nostalgic undertones that set it apart from other genres. Whether it's the static crackle of vinyl or the simplicity of imperfect melodies, these elements together create a soundscape that feels both intimate and expansive.

What stands out the most is how lo-fi music isn't just about sound; it's about an experience. The cultural impact of Lo-fi stretches beyond mere audio enjoyment. It serves as background music for studying, working, or simply unwinding after a long day. It's a soothing backdrop in an increasingly chaotic world.

Now, reflecting on the bigger picture, lo-fi music holds substantial weight in today's musical landscape. It transcends conventional boundaries by fostering a sense of community among listeners and creators alike. The genre's emphasis on inclusivity allows anyone with a basic setup to produce their own tracks. This ethos has cultivated a diverse array of artists who contribute their unique flavors to the genre. It's not just about low-fidelity sounds; it's about high-quality feelings and connections.

The significance of Lo-fi extends to its ability to bridge generational gaps. Older listeners might appreciate its nods to vintage sounds and old-school jazz influences. At the same time, younger fans enjoy its modern twist and relevance to contemporary life. This blend of the old and new creates a timeless appeal that resonates across age groups and cultures.

As we've explored the intricacies of lo-fi music, it's clear this isn't just another trend destined to fade away. Its cultural resonance suggests it's here to stay. The genre's adaptability means it will continue to evolve, absorbing new influences while retaining its core essence. With every beat, scratch, and loop, Lo-fi tells a story that listeners are eager to hear.

So, where do we go from here? Well, I hope that this book doesn't mark the end of your exploration but rather the beginning. Now is the time to dive deeper into the sea of lo-fi music. Explore different subgenres, discover new artists, and perhaps even experiment with creating your own lo-fi tracks. Appreciate the artistry—the careful crafting of each beat, the thoughtful layering of samples, and the subtle imperfections that give Lo-fi its character. Embrace the genre's simplicity, and let it inspire you in your daily life.

Lo-fi music celebrates the unpolished, the raw, and the human. It reminds us that beauty lies in the imperfections and that sometimes, the less polished version can be more meaningful. In a world that often values perfection and high standards, Lo-fi encourages us to slow down, appreciate the moment, and find joy in the little things.

The future of lo-fi music is bright and full of potential. Technological advancements will undoubtedly bring new tools and techniques that artists can leverage to push the boundaries of the genre. However, the soul of Lo-fi—the emphasis on organic sounds and emotional depth—will remain intact. As listeners, we have the privilege of witnessing this evolution unfold. We can look forward to innovative compositions, collaborations across genres, and perhaps even new ways to experience lo-fi music, whether through virtual reality, interactive platforms, or other emerging technologies.

To all the music enthusiasts and adult listeners who've embarked on this journey with us, thank you for your curiosity and passion. May this book serve as a stepping stone in your ongoing exploration of music. Keep listening, keep discovering, and most importantly, keep enjoying the magic of lo-fi music.

In closing, remember that lo-fi music is more than just a genre—it's a movement, a feeling, and an ever-present companion in the soundtrack of our lives. So, sit back, relax, and let the mellow rhythms of Lo-fi continue to soothe your soul.

Glossary

Ambient Sounds: Naturalistic audio elements like rain, wind, and other environmental noises are often incorporated into lo-fi tracks to create a more immersive, atmospheric vibe.

Analog: This refers to the use of physical, continuous electrical signals rather than digital, discrete signals. Analog audio equipment like tape machines and vinyl records is integral to lo-fi sound.

Cassette: A magnetic tape recording format popular in the 20th century, known for its warm, low-fidelity sound quality. Cassette recordings are a hallmark of the lo-fi aesthetic.

Chillhop: A subgenre of Lo-fi that blends laid-back hip-hop beats with jazzy, downtempo melodies and a focus on creating a mellow, contemplative mood.

Chillwave: A genre-blending Lo-fi, Synthwave, and Indie Pop characterized by hazy, nostalgic soundscapes and a laidback, emotive vibe.

Crackle: The audible pops and crackles inherent to playing vinyl records, often emulated in lo-fi productions to evoke a vintage feel.

Crate Digging: The practice of scouring thrift stores, garage sales, and record shops to uncover obscure vinyl treasures that can be sampled and repurposed in lo-fi productions.

Bandcamp: A popular online music platform embraced by the lo-fi community for its artist-friendly policies and support of independent, DIY music.

Bitcrusher: A digital effect that deliberately reduces the bit depth and sample rate of an audio signal, creating a lo-fi, distorted, and gritty sound.

Drum Machines: Old, vintage drum machines like the Roland TR-808 and TR-909 are beloved in lo-fi music for their raw, lo-fi percussion sounds that add grit and character to beats.

Fader Automation: Deliberately manipulating the volume faders during a lo-fi track's recording to create a dynamic, organic feel, as opposed to static, unchanging levels.

Fidelity: The level of audio quality, with lo-fi music placing emphasis on lower fidelity and the preservation of imperfections over technical perfection.

Filtering: Applying low-pass, high-pass, or band-pass filters to audio signals to sculpt the tone and frequencies, resulting in the warm, filtered sound often heard in lo-fi music.

Glitch: Intentionally introducing digital artifacts, stutters, and other "glitchy" imperfections into lo-fi productions to create a more avant-garde, experimental sound.

Granular Synthesis: A technique used in lo-fi music that involves breaking down audio samples into tiny grains and then reshaping and recontextualizing them to create new, atmospheric textures.

Hiss: The constant background noise and tape hiss associated with analog audio equipment, used in lo-fi music to create a warm, lived-in ambiance.

Imperfection: Small, unintended sonic irregularities or "flaws" embraced in lo-fi music as a means of adding character and authenticity.

Lo-fi: Refers to lower-quality audio fidelity, with an emphasis on gritty, raw, and unrefined sonic qualities over technical perfection.

Lo-fi Hip Hop: A subgenre of Lo-fi that blends classic hip-hop elements like dusty beats and soulful samples with the genre's signature warm, hazy aesthetic.

Minimalism: The aesthetic principle of lo-fi music that values simplicity, restraint, and the omission of excessive elements in both production and composition.

Nostalgia: The sense of wistful longing for the past evoked by the vintage sonic qualities and analog imperfections found in lo-fi music.

Pitch Shifting: Deliberately changing the pitch of a sample or recording, either up or down, to create interesting, offbeat melodies and harmonies in lo-fi compositions.

Reverb: Adding artificial reverb, especially the lo-fi reverb found on vintage hardware, which imparts a spacious, atmospheric quality to lo-fi tracks.

Sampling: The practice of incorporating snippets of existing recordings into new musical compositions, a technique commonly used in lo-fi beats and hip-hop.

Tape Loops: By repeatedly recording and playing back segments of audio tape, lo-fi producers create mesmerizing, hypnotic loops that are a hallmark of the genre's production style.

Tape Saturation: The natural compression and harmonic distortion that occurs when an analog tape machine is pushed to its limits, contributing to the warm, fuzzy lo-fi sound.

Vaporwave: An experimental subgenre of electronic music that draws heavily on the lo-fi aesthetic, often repurposing and slowing down 80s/90s pop and elevator music samples.

Vinyl: Analog phonograph records, which are highly influential in lo-fi music for their characteristic pops, crackles, and low-end frequency response.

Vinyl Emulation: Using software or hardware tools to digitally recreate the sonic characteristics of vinyl records, like pops, crackles, and a warmer frequency response.

References

Amable, J. (2019, February). *Chill beats to study/relax to.* JSTOR Daily. https://daily.jstor.org/chill-beats-to-study-relax-to/

Bauer, C., Kowald, D., Lex, E., Reisinger, W., & Schedl, M. (2021, February). *Listener Modeling and Context-aware Music Recommendation Based on Country Archetypes.* Frontiers in Artificial Intelligence. https://www.frontiersin.org/journals/artificial-intelligence/articles/10.3389/frai.2020.508725/full

Criscuolo, I. (2022, November). *What is Lo-Fi Music and Why is it Perfect for Relaxing?.* Domestika. https://www.domestika.org/en/blog/10296-what-is-lo-fi-music-and-why-is-it-perfect-for-relaxing

Darling, M. (n.d.). *Synthesis, Sampling, and Sound Design in Film Scoring: Electronic and Textural Resources.* Berklee Online. https://online.berklee.edu/courses/synthesis-sampling-and-sound-design-in-film-scoring-electronic-and-textural-resources

Harper, A. (2014). *Lo-fi Aesthetics in Popular Music Discourse.* [Doctoral dissertation, Wadham College, University of Oxford] https://www.academia.edu/14978906/Lo_Fi_Aesthetics_in_Popular_Music_Discourse

How to Make a Lo-fi Hip-Hop Beat in Soundtrap. (n.d.). Retrieved from: https://www.deptofsound.org/resource-hub/how-to-make-a-lo-fi-hip-hop-beat-in-soundtrap

Indie Pop: Authentic, Creative, and Full of Energy. (2024, June). *Musiknerd.* https://musiknerd.org/en/music-genre/pop-music/indie-pop/

In Memoriam 2017: The Musicians We Lost. (2017, December). Jefferson Public Radio. https://www.ijpr.org/2017-12-29/in-memoriam-2017-the-musicians-we-lost

Keep It on the Down Lo(-Fi). (n.d.). Retrieved from: https://www.mymcpl.org/blogs/keep-it-down-lo-fi

Krukowski, D. (2017, April). *Surface Noise.* The Paris Review. https://www.theparisreview.org/blog/2017/04/21/surface-noise/

Ledesma, E. (n.d.). *Do Androids Dream of Electric Llamas? AI-*generated *Cinema in Latin America.* Forma. https://www.formajournal.org/ledesma-ai-cinema

Murahari, N., & Pinard, S. (2022, November). Ambient Sounds and Subliminal Layering in Low-Fidelity Music. *Journal of Student Research*, 11(4).

Music Production, Technology, and Innovation. (n.d.). Berklee Remix: Research Media and Information Exchange. Retrieved from: https://remix.berklee.edu/graduate-studies-production-technology/index.7.html

Neal, A. (2022, April). Lo-fi Today. *Organised Sound*, 27(1), 32-40. https://www.cambridge.org/core/journals/organised-sound/article/lofi-today/73B4DDB240C2B2DC0A0E64249AB44325

Origins, M. (2020, April). *The Origins of Lo-fi.* The Music Origins Project. https://musicorigins.org/the-origins-of-lo-fi/

Pearce, S. (2022, December 9). *Sheldon Pearce's Top 20 Albums of 2022.* KHSU. https://www.khsu.org/2022-12-09/sheldon-pearces-top-20-albums-of-2022

Philip Sherburne: Thumbnail Music Redux: Part One. phs.abstractdynamics.org. (n.d.). http://phs.abstractdynamics.org/2009/12/

Roots of Lofi hip hop: Amateur Music Making, Recording Technology, and Globalization. (2022, November). American Culture Studies. https://amcs.wustl.edu/roots-lofi-hip-hop-amateur-music-making-recording-technology-and-globalization

Studying with Music: B*enefits and* T*ips.* (2023, May). Grand Canyon University. https://www.gcu.edu/blog/gcu-experience/studying-music-benefits-and-tips

The Evolution of Lo-fi Hip Hop: A Closer Look. (n.d.). www.projectchambermusic.org. https://www.projectchambermusic.org/the-evolution-of-lo-fi-hip-hop-a-closer-look

The Boar. Theboar.org. (2020). https://theboar.org/2020/05/what-is-lo-fi-music/

Vandentop, E. (2020, October 20). *Lo-Fi Bedroom Pop Artist Senseless Optimism Talks New Music, Geographical Influences, Mental Health, & More.* Music Mecca. http://musicmecca.org/lo-fi-bedroom-pop-artist-senseless-optimism-to-release-new-ep-dreamland-demos/

ZULI: A very M*odern Sampler.* (n.d.). Ecmfa. Retrieved from: http://www.ecmfa-2011.org/index-1071.html

About the Author

Theresa Smith, a native of Brooklyn, New York, was born into a family of musicians and music aficionados, with the sounds of Italian opera accompanying her throughout her childhood. She grew up immersed in music, dedicating her time to the piano. Theresa earned both her Bachelor's and Master's degrees from the University of Connecticut, and music remains an integral part of her life. As a mother of three, two of her children are also musicians, embracing various genres. Her youngest son, Lucas, introduced her to Lo-fi music, leading to a diverse soundscape in their home. Theresa is the author of *Women In Football: Past Present and Future* and was honored as "Teacher of the Year" in 2017 in her New York school district.

Made in the USA
Middletown, DE
28 November 2025

23326498R10086